The Invention of Everything:

Insights on Life, Food, and One Good Thermos

From the Pages of 543 Magazine

Everett De Morier

Blydyn  Square Books

Kenilworth, New Jersey

© 2018 by Everett De Morier

ISBN
978-1-7320156-0-9 (ebook)
978-1-7320156-1-6 (paperback)

CIP information available upon request.

The views, thoughts, and opinions expressed belong solely to the author, and not necessarily to Blydyn Square Books or its associates and/or affiliates.

Cover design by Daniel Wallace
Interior layout and design by Kristin McCarthy

Acknowledgments

Because this book covers many different time periods and many different places, I wanted to thank everyone along the way who inspired its creation.

This, of course, does not include that guy at the bowling alley in Sidney who yelled at me for no reason when I was fourteen.

You, sir, are a total jerk.

But to everyone else—thanks.

Table of Contents

Introduction:

Way Back When

Around the time that I met the woman who would later be my wife—this would have been in the year of our Lord 1990—a twenty-something-year-old me made a radical shift in occupational status. I became—a writer.

Now, this may seem like a big step for a door-to-door salesman for the cable company to take, but it was actually pretty easy and only had two steps.

The first step was simple and involved me identifying as a writer. So, I went to bed one night dreaming of ways sell the HBO and Cinemax combo, and I woke up—ta-da!—a writer. Done. I began calling myself that. Thinking that way. Attaching that title as part of who I was.

And after that was done, the second step was to work the fact that I was now a writer into every possible situation.

"I was going how fast, officer? Wow, I am so sorry. But you know us writers; we are pretty scatter-brained."

"Hey, happy birthday. Instead of a card, I wrote you a little something—seeing that I'm a writer and all. Hold on to that; I signed it."

"A polyp, huh? Wow, that sounds serious. Did I mention that I'm a writer now?"

And that was it. Transition complete.

No forms to fill out, no jobs to quit, and nothing really to do after that.

Now, I know what you're thinking, and the answer is, no. You don't need to be published to be a writer. Or have any formal training. You didn't even need to actually write anything. Ever. You just need to be a writer. It's like a Halloween costume that you never, ever take off.

And life goes on. But it now does so with you as a writer.

But to be fair, occasionally you come across some incredibly rude people and the conversation begins to derail:

"Well, I work for the cable company now, but I'm really a writer."

And then they will ask something incredibly obnoxious: "Oh, that's cool. So, what do you write?"

At first, this may be a stumbling block, but if you are prepared, if you have trained, then you can quickly recover.

"Me? I freelance."

Boom. Back in the saddle. And your life kerchunks along, taking you, the writer, along with it.

And the added bonus is, when you get in trouble at work because of those two-hour lunches you're taking, and when all your friends are buying a house and you are struggling to make rent on your studio apartment—hey, it's not your fault. You shouldn't be working these dead-end jobs anyway. You're a writer! A creative person.

For me, as a writer, life moved on.

Debbie and I got married. I put on a tie and got a job with a desk. And I started to actually write once in a while and even managed to talk a publisher into buying a book of mine. Then I talked them into a second book a few years later. And years after that, a novel came out.

We had two great boys, Nick and Alex, and I worked the title of writer into conversation much less, but I managed to shoehorn the dad status in as often as possible.

"Oh, yeah? I had no idea that Bulgarian yogurt was in such high demand. But did I tell you the crazy thing one of my kids said the other day?"

Being a father became not only another way to be creative, but the best kind. My kids were my audience and I focused on teaching them the things that I was taught—how to use a hammer, how to build a fire—showing my sons the skills that young men need to know and doing it the way that I learned it all myself, not just by instruction, but through stories.

Because you can't learn how to gap a sparkplug unless you know how the sparkplug was first invented. You can't learn how to pack a suitcase unless you know about the guy in Luxembourg who taught me the greatest packing secrets ever.

And when I tried to organize all of these tips, to make sure I didn't miss any of this great stuff, I'd add a few more items to the list, and then a few more after that. There were hundreds and hundreds of things that every man should know: how to jumpstart a car, how to choose a watch, how to tie a tie. And all this information eventually became the website 543skills.com.

I launched the site and it quickly developed a following. As it grew in popularity, it also expanded in scope. So much so, that I couldn't do it alone, and so, I found a partner: a tech-savvy guy named Daniel Wallace who not only knew where all the bits and bytes should go, but how all that design and layout stuff worked.

Yes, the site talked about how to cook on a charcoal grill, but we also presented articles on what willpower really is. The site discussed soldering irons, as well as where confidence comes from.

And when we began to look at the emails coming in from readers of the site, when we started to review the growing mailing list, we saw that there were just as many women visiting the site as men.

So, Daniel and I rebranded and relaunched. *543 Skills* became *543 Magazine*—with a new look, a new feel, and a new slogan. Instead of "All the Skills a Man Needs to Know," it was now "Skills, Tips, and Insight." Not just for men—for everyone.

And the site moved on.

And one day, when I was having lunch with my publisher—which by the way, is the absolutely coolest phrase to ever get to say:

"Chopped salad? Oh yeah, I had that at lunch with my publisher."

"Wednesday? No, that won't work; I'm having lunch with my publisher."

"What do you mean, I cut you off? My publisher will hear about this. Right after lunch. Which I'm having with her. Today. Moron."

During one of these powerful lunches that people like me have, we started talking about 543 and began to toss around the idea of turning it into a book. What if we collected pieces from the online magazine and translated them into a book and wrote some new stuff?

And that's what we did. And now you're all caught up.

So welcome to *The Invention of Everything: Insights on Life, Food, and One Good Thermos*—the book version of the site, with a few extra things added in.

Thanks for reading it.

Everett De Morier
A Funny Way of Looking at It
https://everettdemorier.com/

Skill #523:

How to Make Pickled Eggs

There are several symbols of life that have pretty much vanished from the American landscape. These include payphones, Western Union telegrams, and video rental stores. Gone are the days when you would go to the hardware store to use the machine to test your television tubes in order to determine which ones needed replacing—eliminating those expensive TV repairmen who charged an arm and a leg.

Yup. Those days are pretty much over.

Another casualty of modern living is something missing from the neighborhood bar. At one time, back by the cash register, there near the packs of cigarettes and the book where they kept track of your weekly sign-in, you would always see it: that gallon jar of pickled eggs. Beautiful, inviting, and glimmering with a vinegary glow.

The local bar's pickled egg had been a staple for decades. It often provided the only solid food a working man would have before heading home after a hard day. Originally, the bar egg was simply a hardboiled egg, offered free to patrons the way pretzels are today, in order to make customers thirstier—and also to keep them from getting sloppily drunk. But health concerns grew and this practice migrated to selling just the pickled version of eggs, which lasted longer (and eliminated the need to clean up all those eggshells!).

The pickled egg first showed up on the American scene in the 1700s, and although many believe the eggs to be a British transplant, it was actually the German colonists who brought pickled eggs with them. The eggs were popular with Hessian mercenaries and then migrated over to the Pennsylvania Dutch, who used a very simple practice to make them: The egg—or the cucumber or the beet, whatever they were pickling—was placed in a jar of spiced vinegar and left there.

If pickling hasn't quite become a lost art, it has definitely become a niche one and is often lumped in with canning. Which is not accurate.

Canning is the act of preserving food for storage. Pickling is when vinegar and spices infuse the food and alter its structure.

Can a tomato and you still have a tomato. But pickle an egg and you get something completely different.

Pickling any food is pretty easy. It doesn't require special canning pots and jars and can be done with just a few leftover glass jars and a pot—I mean, you can use all that fancy stuff if you have it, but it's not required.

Because you can easily pickle eggs—or sausage or anything—with items that are just lying around the average house, it's easy. It's fun and it's one of those aspects of cooking that everyone believes is a lot more difficult than it really is. And you can be very creative with pickling because the flavor changes with not only the spices, but also with whatever else you pickle with the egg or other food you're making—hot peppers or fruit or whatever else you add in.

Plus, there is this unique effect that happens when you bring homemade pickled eggs to a barbecue or an event: You move up a few rungs on the unique-ladder—depending on how narrow-minded and culinary-retentive your friends are, it's possible that no one may eat your eggs. But I guarantee there won't be three other jars of pickled eggs at the tailgate.

Now, the one downside to pickled eggs is that pickling doesn't preserve the eggs for the long term the way canning preserves food. Commercial pickled eggs can be kept on a shelf for years, but homemade ones need to be refrigerated even before they are opened.

And the very first—and really, the only—rule of any pickling endeavor is: Don't use prepackaged pickling spices. I have tried these before and they are basically salt with some more salt added in for flavor. You can create a much, much better pickling brine on your own.

The most difficult aspect of pickling eggs has nothing to do with the cooking part—it's getting those eggs out of their shells. Unpeeling hardboiled eggs is tedious and yields completely inconsistent results, so here are a few tricks that work pretty well.

The Baking Soda Method
If you increase the pH of the water in which you're cooking the egg, the shell will actually break down. So, add in half a teaspoon of baking soda for every quart of water you use. Boil the eggs for twelve to fifteen minutes—you want to make sure it's hard-cooked. Let cool and peel.

The Lung Power Method
Here's how it's supposed to work: First, crack the shell at the very top and bottom of the egg, then peel off about a dime-sized hole on each end. Next, place your mouth over the hole on the top of the egg and blow. According to some very cool YouTube videos, this should work—but I have only made it work if I used the baking soda method first.

The Crack-All-Over Method

Take the egg and crack both top and bottom and then, on a paper towel, roll the egg around and crack the entire surface. You'll know you've done this when you stop hearing the cracking sound. If you've done it right, the shell should come off in large pieces. I've had this work many times—and not work many times. The key seems to be that older eggs peel better. Newer ones—especially the ones my wife gets directly from her friends who have chickens—are a pain to peel.

The Swirl Method

The philosophy here is, you cook the eggs, remove them, and place them in a pot with a few inches of cold water. Then, in the pot, swirl the eggs in a circle, letting the eggs bump and crack and slam against one another. When you take the eggs out, they should be partially unpeeled and easy to finish. I have tried this method and it works sometimes. It makes a mess—but you do get a great forearm workout.

The Glass of Water Method

This is my go-to method for unpeeling hardboiled eggs. I use it all the time. You place the egg in a glass with an inch or so of water in it. Cover the top with your hand and shake it and swirl it. The eggshell will take on small cracks over the surface and the water will get in between the shell and help it slip right off.

Making Pickled Eggs

So, now that the eggs are peeled, you are ready to start pickling.

Step one is to find a jar that can be sealed tightly—leftover pickle jars or anything with a wide mouth and a lid that seals will work. A quart-size canning jar will hold about a dozen medium-sized eggs. Clean the jar thoroughly.

Put the eggs and the extras—which can include cut-up onion, sweet peppers, hot peppers, garlic cloves, whatever you want—inside the jar.

In a large pan, add three-quarters of a cup of water, a cup and a half of apple cider vinegar, three teaspoons of salt, two teaspoons of sugar, one clove of garlic, some dill, mustard seed, or any other spices you want—there are no rules.

Bring the pot to a boil and let it simmer for five minutes.

Right before you are ready to pour everything into the jar, run hot water over the outside surface of the jars you are using to warm them up—you don't want them to crack.

Pour the mixture into the jar and cover with the lid.

That's it.

So, pickle yourself up some eggs. Then sit down with the racing form, pour yourself a Genesee Cream Ale, and let everyone know how you feel about the energy crisis and those new pocket calculators that everyone's talking about.

This is still America after all.

The Story of Eric

Eric tossed the bag in the wheelbarrow as if it were just an afterthought, an impulse, instead of what it really was— a sixty-pound bag of cement—and it hit the metal wheelbarrow with a thud. Even the wheelbarrow shuddered from the impact, but Eric didn't seem to be affected by the task. He picked up his shovel and pierced the sharp end into the bag—which was disappointing because that was becoming my favorite part—then we pulled out the pieces of bag and I added in water from the hose.

"You two are a mess."

We were both caked with mud and sweat when Debbie's phone made that shutter sound as she snapped a picture.

"The word you're looking for is not mess," I corrected her, through heavy breaths. "It's macho."

"That's right," Eric agreed, stirring the cement with his shovel. "We are about as manly as it gets."

Debbie placed the phone back in her pocket because Debbie only takes one picture of anything. Just one. In a world of digital photography, when you can take dozens of shots, increasing the odds of capturing a few treasures, she makes just a single pass at it.

Debbie could stumble across Elvis coming out of a spaceship shaking hands with Jimmy Hoffa and Bigfoot, and she would excitedly pull out her phone and take one photograph. Click. Then, hours later, when she was trying to post that picture—which would be of the spaceship stairs because that would be all she caught—she would actually have the nerve to be disappointed. And this is the reason that the one and only photograph of Eric and me pouring the footers for our new deck is actually of both of our backs.

"I'll take more pictures later," she said.

And there would be chances to take those pictures. Once the footers were dry, Eric and I would start on the frame and there would be additional pictures—of our eyes closed, our feet, and a few of the dog—there is always a need for new pictures of the dog. And because pictures of Eric were not at a premium—because he wasn't dead and it looked like he would remain not-dead for a long time—there would be time for these other photographs.

Eric is not supposed to be just dead; he's supposed to be long dead. By almost a year. In fact, that's why he came here and that's why he ended up living two houses away from us. He came here to die.

The details of Eric's life before we met him aren't completely clear to me and I haven't asked. The basic fact is that when he arrived here, he was diagnosed as terminal. When the doctors said there was no hope, he called his family to say good-bye and that was when his sister Dianne moved him up from Florida to spend his last few weeks in Dover, Delaware, with her and her family.

"I didn't want my brother to die alone," Dianne would say with a smile, her eyes tired.

But Eric in those early days was not the Eric I know today. That Eric was a skeleton in a red bathrobe who would walk in his front yard to smoke a cigarette and would nod if cornered, but nothing else. He was gaunt, beaten, broken, and sleeping in a borrowed bed while the loan he had on life was about to come due.

When the doctors said it was time, hospice workers came to the house. They made him comfortable. They said Eric would be gone in a week. The next week, they said it would be the following week. Then they said a month. Then they stopped coming and told Dianne to call them as soon as Eric was dead.

She said she would.

More months went by, and Eric's travels from the house became longer. He took short walks. Then he took longer ones. Then he bought a used bicycle and could be seen pedaling along back streets. Even his conversations got longer—on his front lawn, always in that red bathrobe. And any topic was fascinating and new.

I didn't know Eric before he came here, so I don't know if that childlike excitement he suddenly seemed to have was the real him or if it was the reaction of a man who had been given a second chance and didn't want to waste a single moment of it. But the Eric I know, now, is easygoing and inquisitive.

"Looks like rain," Eric said as he covered the two footers with a tarp and we tipped the wheelbarrows over them for additional protection. Then we walked the tools to his truck.

"This is a great truck." I shut the tailgate.

"I know." Eric beamed. "Did I tell you I got it for fifteen hundred?"

"No," I lied.

And I got to hear the story again.

The deck has been finished now for over five years—it even had to be pressure-washed a few times. We practically live out there from April to October.

And speaking of living, so is Eric. Still.

He's moved now, so I don't see him as much as I used to. He has a small contractor business and keeps busy—but not too busy. He never takes on work that would get in the way of what is truly important: fishing.

He goes all the time.

And whenever I walk out on our deck, the deck that Eric and I built, I always think of what happens when what the experts say is different from what life says. Plenty of smart people said that Eric was going to die. But life had other plans for him.

So, as always, life wins.

Skill #52:

The Lost Art of Eye Contact

My son's best friend, Austin, practically grew up at our house. He is all grown up now and lives in Seattle, but all through high school, he pretty much lived here. He ate here a few times a week. He slept over once or twice a month. When we went on trips, we took him along and when his parents were looking for him, the first place they checked was our family room, where he and my son Nick would be laughing through some interactive battle that required headsets and game controllers.

Then, one day—for about a week—Austin just stopped showing up.

Nick was still in the family room—talking to unseen people in the world of Xbox Live—but no one else was there.

When my wife asked where Austin was, Nick gave us a confused look, then answered, "Home." And it was then that we understood what had happened.

Austin had been saving his money and just got his own Xbox. So, now, Nick and his friend were spending the same amount of time together, talking on headsets and playing the same interactive games, blowing up the same creatures that exploded party favors out of their heads when they were killed, only now his friend was plugged in at his own house and Nick was plugged in here.

The frightening aspect of this was: They were both perfectly fine with it.

The key was for the two of them to be together in the world of *Minecraft*. They didn't need to physically be in the same room, just as long as they were both in the game at the same time.

Now, when Austin was sixteen, he had a girlfriend. She lived in Canada. He lived in Delaware. They sent emails, texts, and talked during the week. They got each other Christmas presents and birthday presents and had been dating for over a year. However, they had never met in real life. They discovered each other somewhere online and viewed themselves as being in a serious relationship.

The fact that they had never met was not a concern for either one of them. And when I asked, "How can you be dating someone you have never physically seen?" Austin would smile and give me a patient "Wow, you are so old" look.

The point of all of this is that we live at an extremely unique point in technological history. For the first time, we can discuss, fight, negotiate, schedule, console, beg, mend, and comfort without ever actually needing the person with whom we are communicating to be anywhere even remotely near us.

On any given day, we text, phone, email, Facebook, Bluetooth, chat, play interactive games, and Tweet more than we interface directly, face-to-face, with other people.

The process goes like this: We interact with a device—a cell phone, a keyboard, an iPad, a game controller, a Bluetooth headset—and then wait for the people with whom we're corresponding—someone we usually cannot even see—to interact with their devices and reply back. The gadgets we are using are near us. But the people we're transmitting to are not.

Now, before you roll your eyes and think this is going to be a rant against technology, let me clarify: I'm not railing against modernity; I'm simply demonstrating two things: The first is that we have become extremely comfortable communicating without actual human contact, through a device. And second, given the choice, many of us often prefer to communicate in this fashion.

Austin was a smart and good-looking kid—tall, blond, on the school swimming team—and yet he was content with a girlfriend who lived a thousand miles away, a girl he could date only through a keyboard or cell phone, rather than one he could actually interact with.

Here's another example.

You are in a restaurant and see a group of people sitting at a table together—and this is not necessarily always a younger group; I've seen people of all ages do this. At least one of these people will be speaking into a cell phone to someone who is not at the table. And we're not talking about a quick five- or ten-second conversation, where there is crucial information that needs to be passed on. I've seen—and heard—thirty-minute casual cell-phone conversations, during dinner, while the people on the phone are sitting and eating at a table with different people.

These individuals had a choice: They could talk to the people sitting directly right in front of them or they could use a device to communicate with someone else who was not even there.

You see this on a massive scale at any airport. There, you will see thousands of people plugged into cell-phone conversations, completely oblivious to the other people who are mere inches away from them, who are also plugged into their own, separate conversations.

Maybe they're busy? Maybe these are very busy businesspeople closing crucial and important deals.

Maybe.

But it's not hard to listen to a sampling of most of these calls—many people on cell phones don't seem to realize that sound travels—and know that they are, in large part, mundane and simply chatty. Actually, most times, the calls simply seem to be a way to kill time.

And even though the content of the calls is usually noncritical, the need to stay connected to other individuals is extremely great.

I was amazed the first time I was in a busy airport men's room and saw a man continue his cell-phone conversation as he stepped into a bathroom stall—better yet, he actually took a new call while he was already in there. Nowadays, this kind of thing happens so often, I don't even notice.

A month ago, at the gym, a man stepped into the shower and hung his shorts—with his cell phone in the pocket—on the hook outside the shower curtain. His phone rang and he reached his wet hand out to get his phone—and took the call while in the shower.

So, what's the point of all this?

It's simply this:

We are so accustomed to communicating with people without seeing them—and our need to do so is so great—that we no longer see the people who are actually present all around us.

The people who are ancillary to our daily lives—the toll-both operator, the cashier, the waitress—simply become white noise. They are nothing more than a disjointed voice and therefore don't require our attention—and we are now very used to talking to disjointed voices. We say hello, we say thank you, we leave, and we rarely—very, very rarely—make eye contact. The people around us are unimportant.

Up until recently, if you entered a crowded room of strangers, that room and those strangers became your world.

Until you left that room, those people were connected to you simply because you were sharing the same space, the same situation, the same time.

No more.

Now, we can be in the same room but be texting someone else, making a phone call, or sending an email from our phone. The physical space we occupy is no longer important. We are no longer in the same room as the person just a few feet away from us because we are now connected to someplace else and therefore we are disconnected from the people right next to us.

But what does all this have to do with eye contact?

Eye contact is a tricky area anyway and now—because of the change in technological culture—it is becoming even more complex. We use eye contact to seduce as well as to intimidate. We use it to calm and to ignite. The wrong look at the wrong time can lead to a battle. The right look at the right time can lead to love.

Eye contact is a tool. A weapon. An open door to who we really are. And instead of learning to use it properly, we shut it down. We allow it to grow dull and rusty. And we forget about it.

Austin has a great life on the other side of the country now. He has roommates he met while gaming, a job he found online, and he and Nick text all the time. In fact, Austin was in Nick's wedding this past spring.

So, technology has definitely aided in his world and will continue to do so for years to come.

But I guarantee you that there are many eyes in Austin's world that he's never seen, never made contact with. And maybe this isn't a bad thing.

And maybe it is.

The Midlife Review

When you begin to climb the years past fifty, the viewpoint changes. The ego dwindles but the curiosity grows. And you start to wonder. To think. To plan all the things that need to be done and to squeeze them in to the time you have left to do them.

But not the things you have to do for you, because you start to care less about those. Instead, you think more about all there is to do for the people around you.

It has been fifty years.
Well, no—that's not true.
Once you carry the seven,
it's been fifty-two.
And in fifty-two years,
no vast rise or succumb.
Slower than many,
but brighter than some.

So now, halfway through,
time, the older man's chore:
to weigh and assess,
all I need answer for.
Not a trial, inquisition,
or a stern talking to,
but a chance to appraise.
It's my midlife review.

So, I found a nice tie,
a clean shirt, and a coat.
And I drove to the place,
spelled out there on the note,
to a part of the city
not been to before.
I walked to the building
and right through the door.

Once inside the office,
I strode down the aisle,
where a man at a desk
sat reading my file.
He stood and bowed, hi,
rolled to me a chair.
On the walls, the photos—
those before me—hung there.

Then he spoke with a smile:
Well, I've good news to tell.
On your choice of a spouse,
you did quite very well.
She is loving, supportive,
and in church, volunteers.
Did not kill you, not once,
in all twenty-three years.

Then stirring through papers,
to find the right page:
On your kids, here again,
mostly high marks to gauge.
Sons are happy and strong,
tender hearts they have grown;
both to soon make their marks,
they can think on their own.

But now, that part over,
smile fading from face,
he shuffled the papers.
Let's get back to your case.
In the asset department,
you must surely know,
that your financial levels
are shockingly low.

I smirked and replied,
mine's more lofty pursuit.
Don't you know that with evil
it's money at root?
As you see, it's my family,
the center for me—
not the stocking of wealth,
here in this life, agree?

Then he took off his glasses,
and then rubbed his nose.
I think there's confusion,
we should here dispose.
See, the standard for this life's
not to wealth to be driven,
but to be the good stewards
of all we've been given.

And I see by these files
that you've wasted a lot.
Some, they make more of,
but time—they do not.
So, the question remains,
although here not bereft.
Now what will you do
with the twenty years left?

Just twenty? I mocked.
That seems a bit lean.
Well, he said, rounding,
it's more like eighteen.
You will die on a Wednesday,
the fifteenth of May.
Which is eighteen years,
one month, from today.

What? I said, shocked,
as I let this sink in.
I know, this is hard,
but we must now begin.
You need to make plans,
to ponder in thought.
So, what will you do
with the years you've still got?

And I sat in that chair
with my heart in a twist
'til I finally did speak.
Well, I do have a list.
But before I could finish,
he stopped me there, true.
This gift you've received,
it's not about you.

You've been handed this grant,
not to ski down a slope,
not to climb up a mountain,
or zip down a rope.
You came into this world
with nothing you own,
and all that you have
is simply on loan.

And soon on a day,
eighteen years from now,
you will stand before Him
to answer your vow.
And when that linking
from this world is free,
what for the kingdom
did you do for Me?

He handed me pamphlets
and wished me good luck.
And I dazedly shuffled
right back to my truck.
And I sat there inside,
letting set that review.
So little time,
and so much to do.

How to Shine Your Shoes

Although the good old days when shoeshine boys stood on street corners—young kids with a shoe box, offering a quick shine to passersby—were well before my time, I did get to be part of the great suit era of the 1980s, when, no matter whether you worked in the mailroom or had the corner office, you donned a suit and tie.

And that was also a time of shoeshine guys.

Those shoeshine guys—with their barbershop-like chairs on a pedestal—were everywhere: hotels, airports, even some restaurants. Which made perfect sense because those were the days when your first impression was determined by the firmness of your handshake and the shine of your shoes.

Now, if you think shoeshine guys were just a nostalgic throwback to a different era, I guess they were. But for many young men, a shoeshine represented a rite of passage. Having your shoes professionally shined while you sat there and looked on meant that you were not only old enough to get your shoes shined—and were actually wearing shoes that could be shined, not sneakers—but that you could pay for it yourself. For a few bucks, you could feel both responsible and frivolous at the same time.

They are mostly gone now, the shoeshine guys. I mean, you still see them in airports and most major cities still have them, but the bulk of them—the shoeshine guys who set up as you waited to get a table for lunch or while you sat at a bus stop—are gone. Most of us are wearing business casual now, and our loafers don't seem to need to be as shiny as our wingtips did back in the day.

Most likely, the next generation probably won't need the shoeshine guys like we did. They have their own rites of passage to go through. But still—even if it's just for a wedding, funeral, or interview—you will find a need to shine your shoes—even if you have to do it yourself. And when you do, you'll want those leather shoes of yours to glow.

Here's how you do it:

Remove the laces of the shoes. A lot of people don't bother with this, but it's the only way to get the tongue of the shoes polished and get in all the nooks and crannies. Take the laces out and fold the tongue up—this is also a good time to replace the laces, if needed.

Clean the shoe—not polish, but clean. Place your hand inside the shoe, and with the other hand, take a slightly damp cloth and wipe down the entire surface of the shoe to get off all the dirt and dust. Note: If you skip this step, you could not only polish the dirt into the leather, but any sort of particle of dust could easily scratch the surface of the shoe.

Apply polish. Using circular motions, apply a thick coat of polish all over the shoe. Don't be stingy here. Get a thick coat of polish all over the shoe and work it in.

Get the shoes wet. With a spray bottle or just by taking your hand through the stream of water from the sink, cover the shoes with beads of water. It's best to do only one shoe at a time. Once the shoe is wet, get in there and start buffing. This is the shining stage. Work it hard and add more water if you need it.

There is this strange pride thing that occurs when you shine your own shoes. Yeah, I know, they're just shoes, but it goes beyond that. Your shoeshine stays hidden, unnoticed, until you look down at your feet during that interview that isn't going so well or that meeting where you feel like you don't belong, and you see that black or brown leather glow. And you think, yeah, I did that.

Yes, it's tiny. But it's there.

You Choose

In Oneonta, New York, on the corner of Main and Church streets, there once sat a bar that I worked in during college called Red's Filling Station. Now, this was a great place. The outside was covered in red-painted stone. The inside had walls and ceilings filled with vintage gas pumps, motorcycles, and license plates—long before the TGI Friday's style became so common.

Red's wasn't named for the color of the building but for the owner, a crotchety upstater who breezed in once a week to complain about the ice usage and sign our paychecks. It was the loudest, craziest, and most popular watering hole in that part of the Catskills, and it was where several of my friends and I worked as bartenders one summer.

One night—this would have been somewhere in July or August 1985—my roommate Kurt, who also worked there, and I realized that, well, not only was our rent due the next day, but collectively we were eighty-four dollars short. So, we came up with a plan—a quick and creative plan that had only one moving part: We would make all the money we needed that night in tips. And we would do it by simply telling the customers exactly how much we wanted them to tip us.

The doors opened, our shift began, and soon the bar was three-feet deep with summer college kids and townies, all clamoring to get drinks.

I went first.

"Okay, two beers." I set the drinks down on the bar in front of the guy in the Sammy Hagar T-shirt. "That'll be a buck-fifty for the beer and a dollar tip. So, two-fifty total."

Sammy Hagar dropped the cash on the bar and made way for the next customer.

"Okay," Kurt yelled out. "Here ya go. Two vodka cranberries and a Molson. Four-fifty and with the tip that will be six bucks."

It went on like this for an hour, until we had made the eighty-four bucks we needed. Then we went back to allowing the customers to decide how much to tip us—and the remainder of the night wasn't as prosperous.

What's interesting is that no one—not one single person—questioned us. No one complained. And no one tipped less (or more) than we told them to.

Now, this is just a story I tell at barbecues and over lunches, but it's important here because it frames the next story—the important one.

Fast-forward about fifteen years. I was now married, we had bought our first house, and we were raising our two small sons in a town called Vestal, New York. For ten years, I made a living in industrial computer electronics—which is a fancy way to say that I befriended corporate buyers and tried to talk them into buying more from me and less from my competition. And life was good.

Then, as the electronics industry began to shift heavily offshore, I felt the pinch. And in May 1999, I received the first of the two layoffs I've had in my career.

I wasn't really concerned about this layoff. I had received job offers from competitors fairly often, so I just contacted them. But by then, everyone was feeling the shift in the industry and these contacts were scrambling to hold on to their own jobs.

With the severance I received, along with unemployment, we could just take care of the essentials—if we tightened our belts a bit. So we did. And I made the job hunt my full-time position, leaving early and coming home late.

During this time, one company made me an interesting proposal. Like everyone else, the company had a hiring freeze in place. If I would agree to work for commission only—covering my own hotel, gas, and expenses and receiving a commission on new business—I could start right away.

It wasn't ideal. Money would go out before it came back in and even if I sold something the first day, it would be months before the commission followed. But it kept me in front of customers, making new contacts, and in the industry, so I agreed.

A few months went by and a little money was trickling in, but not much. Then, the vice president of sales was retiring and had hired his replacement. They were both flying in to Rochester to introduce the new VP to one of our largest customers. My job was to make the three-hour drive to pick them up at the airport, go to the meeting, and then get them back to the airport. The thing was, I could tell by the phone conversations of the past week that the honeymoon was over and our relationship would soon end.

When the plane landed, I was there to pick them up.

"Well, we should probably start with the real reason you're here and get that out of the way first," I said, in a friendly tone.

They both laughed this off. I was wrong. They had no interest in making any changes, and in fact, I was doing a great job. The hour and a half drive from the airport to the meeting was light and cordial.

We had our meeting. It went well, as did the working lunch after. Then we began the long drive back to the airport.

When we had about forty minutes left to the airport, the mood changed. They started talking about how their expectations were higher than what I was hitting. Was I really giving this my full attention? I hadn't set up as many new customers as they'd been hoping. They weren't sure this was working for them. So, they were canceling our agreement—which would have been fine, except that then they started to get angry. The atmosphere started to intensify and even get threatening.

As the anger built up on their end, I felt myself move into defense mode—offering to listen and apologize, brainstorm, work harder, make sacrifices and . . .

And then something clicked. In a brief moment of lucidness, everything snapped into place and became absolutely clear.

I knew then the difference between what *I had to do* and what *I didn't have to do*. Everything stopped and I knew what my options were. Without anger, without emotion, I put on my turn signal and worked the car toward the far-right lane.

"What are you doing?" the older VP snapped.

"I'm going home," I said, in a calm and almost sleepy tone. "So, I'll let you guys out here."

There was a moment of quiet, then a laugh. "Very funny," he said. Then he pointed down the road and gave the new VP in the backseat one of those "Don't worry; I've got this under control" kind of looks.

But I continued to move the car to the right and then to the side of the highway. Then I stopped.

"Okay, okay," the new VP joined in from the back. "I can understand you're upset. Let's talk about it. Let's head back to the airport and sit down and—"

"I'm not upset," I said as I put the car in park. "I'm not upset at all. This isn't working for either of us. But I also don't have to take you to the airport."

This idea confused them. What did I mean? Of course I had to take them to the airport. What kind of a lunatic was I? I had to take them to the airport. Didn't I see that?

"You have to—"

"No, I don't," I said, and still there was not a single trace of anger in me. "I don't have to and I don't want to. So I'm not going to."

Several moments of frustrated silence followed before anyone spoke.

"Well," the current VP finally said, with a cocky smirk, "then we have an issue because we're not getting out of the car."

"That's fine," I replied. "But I'm turning around at the U-turn spot right up there. And then I'm heading the three hours home, in the opposite direction. So, if you want to get to the airport, this is the closest you'll be."

More silence. More looks back and forth. Then I pressed the button that popped the trunk. They both sat there. Quietly. The old VP got out of the car and the new one followed. I let them get their bags from the trunk and shut it. Then I pulled out, turned the car around, and headed home. I never saw or heard from either one of them again.

Now, do I feel bad for leaving a sixty-five-year-old man and his overweight successor on the side of Highway 90 in the middle of the summer?

Nope. Not at all.

They both had cell phones—granted, back then they were the size of hoagie rolls and cost about three dollars a minute to use, but they could have called someone.

I take no pride in the act of leaving them, only in clearly seeing what my options were. The point was that I didn't have to drive them to the airport, and I didn't want to. So I didn't. I made a choice instead of following the momentum.

I also have no bitterness or anger toward them—I didn't then and I don't now. Because it's not about anger. It's about options.

Because there is nothing in life—and I mean absolutely nothing—that we *have to do.*

We don't *have to* go to work. We don't *have to* make our car payment. We don't *have to* pay taxes, and we don't even *have to* get out of bed in the morning. We *choose* to do all those things.

Now, are there repercussions if we don't do them? Yes. Of course there are. But there is a cause and effect in all things.

Yes, we can make bad choices, and we all do. Every day. But the challenge is to make sure they are our choices, not just our reactions.

Choose to do it, or choose not to. These are the only options. Never do something simply because the bartender tells you to, or because the guy going to the airport needs a lift—it's not your fault that those two idiot bartenders didn't budget for their rent or that the two businessmen didn't want to spring for a rental car.

You determine if you want to tip them or give them a ride.

You decide. And then you choose.

Skill #431:

How to Build a Fire

Barbra Streisand, Ricky Gervais, Daniel Radcliffe, Tina Fey, Barbara Walters. What do they all have in common?

Well, they are all successful, recognizable names in their own fields, but there is something else that binds them together.

Ready?

None of them can drive a car.

These are very prosperous, highly motivated people who have achieved so much in their lives, but they have never mastered one of the skills that most of us learn at sixteen years old. Now, some of this has to do with living in places like London or New York, where driving is actually a detriment, but in some cases, it is simply about not having an interest in driving.

So, can you be successful without learning to drive a car? Yup. Sure. You can work around it.

And can you go through life without knowing how to build a fire? Yup. Sure. You can work around that, too.

But there will come a time—whether it's in the woods, in a cabin, or even in a survival situation—where you might need to. And knowing how means you don't have to ask someone for a ride.

The Golden Rule of Building a Fire

There is one thing that is the single most important part of building a fire and the one that has the most impact. It's also the first rule that most people ignore. It's the fact that you are *building* a fire: not starting one, arranging one, or finding one. Building one.

I've been on camping trips where I've seen guys throw a pile of sticks on the ground, light it, and then get frustrated when a fire doesn't magically appear.

You are building a fire. Constructing it. You are creating a layer of easily combustible material that can be lit easily and will then light other, slightly larger material, which will then light slightly larger material in a precise manner so that heat is created and larger pieces of wood can be burned. This is a construction project, not cooking.

Don't be in a hurry. Take your time and get the foundation done and the fire will happen.

Years ago, I was on a two-day survival weekend with a group of people on Hiawatha Island in New York, and one of our challenges was to build a fire with a battery and steel wool and then get a can of water to boil. As soon as the timer began—we were all racing against each other—we all scrambled to get materials. Now, the guy who actually lit his fire last, the one who spent the most time on the construction of the fire, was the one who succeeded in boiling the water first. His fire went up quickly and efficiently and he actually worked less on the maintenance of the fire because his foundation was so solid.

Building a Fire

Whether you're building a fire in a fireplace, a pit, a stove, or a camp, the rules are all the same. You will need three types of wood:

Tinder—pine needles, paper, dry leaves, dried grass, birch bark

Kindling—small sticks under one inch in diameter, pinecones, bark, wood shavings

Fuel—sticks larger than one inch in diameter

Your tinder goes in the basement of your construction project, the kindling above it, and then the fuel either above that or added on once the fire gets going. Here's the procedure:

Loosely pile the tinder in the center of fire pit or on your fire grate/stove. Be sure air can flow in; the fire needs oxygen for fuel.

Add the kindling around the tinder so when it catches it can ignite the kindling. Two ways to do this are to make it into the shape of a teepee—best for campfires—or a frame, where you have large pieces off to the side and the kindling in the center. You can place the fuel on the edge, but don't rush it; you can always add the fuel when the kindling is hot.

Light the tinder.

Add more tinder as the fire grows. You want the flame to be high at first so the fire catches.

Then add more kindling: The rule of thumb is to get twice as much as you think you need. Remember that kindling is more important than fuel. Getting the fire hot means you can add larger (and even wetter) pieces later, but not getting it hot means you run the risk that the fire will go out.

Add fuel.

Experiment and play around. Building a fire should be something you're confident doing. It may come in pretty handy someday.

The Ballad of Eddie Elbows

When the rest of the troops scattered into the woods during the attack, Edwin De Morier headed for a barn and took shelter there. When he accidentally knocked the oil lamp onto the barn floor—this would have been in France in March 1918—it took only seconds for the flames to race across the straw and up the dry wooden walls. Within minutes, the barn was ablaze.

During the confusion of battle, the fire was all the British and Americans needed to triangulate and regroup. It also increased morale when the three German soldiers who were hiding in the barn loft jumped out and surrendered.

So, could you say that my grandfather was a World War I hero? Umm, sure. Sure, you could.

And because the war was over less than nine months later, it's obvious that Edwin's contributions were a large part of the victory. A very large part. But it's more important to note that the barn fire led to Edwin's one and only nickname: Eddie Elbows.

When Eddie returned home, he went back to his little barbershop in Afton, New York. And after watching Louise Kramer walk past his front window to the hotel she worked at each day, his newfound battlefield bravery allowed him to approach her and say hello—after seventeen failed attempts.

A courtship eventually followed, and a year later, Eddie and Louise were married. They moved into the three rooms above the barbershop.

On February 15, 1923, Louise De Morier gave birth to their first child, a boy named Lawrence, who would always be known as Larry. My father. Three years later, their second child, Lyle, was born.

Life in Afton was happy and carefree, with the exception of Eddie's emphysema, which became more and more severe—leading the shop to be closed more than it was open. And when his clientele began to frequent more reliable barbers, even when he could work, Eddie was seeing less and less business. The family income was dwindling.

In 1936, Larry came home with two announcements for his parents. The first was that he had quit school and the second was that he was now an employee of the D&H Railroad. And although Eddie Elbows and Louise weren't happy about this, the family's options were slim. So, when he was sixteen years old, my father became the sole breadwinner for his parents, his thirteen-year-old brother, and himself. He'd be working alongside men, repairing rail, laying ties, and loading freight.

After 1941, when the United States got involved in World War II, Larry De Morier was one of the first in the area to receive his draft notice. He reported for duty, went through the physical, and after failing the eye exam miserably, was asked by the doctor, "Where are your glasses?"

"Glasses? I don't have any glasses."

"Well, go get glasses, ya idiot. Yer blind as a bat."

Larry was told to see an eye doctor for glasses and wait to be called back for active duty.

The call never came.

I often wonder how my father's life—and ours—would have been different if he had gone to war. Would he have come back? Or, when he did, would he have been more cautious? Would the events that happened to him later not have occurred, or would his training have prepared him to defend himself?

The major turning point, the single event that changed my father's life, occurred in July 1955. Larry walked his mother to the stands of the Afton Fair, where a dog show was being held. He told his mother he would pick her up in an hour when the show was over and he left to explore the fairgrounds on his own.

If Larry had stayed with the crowd or walked down the midway around the animal displays, his life might not have drastically changed.

But he didn't.

He walked in the dark alleyway between the games and the concessions. Seeing him take this path—and believing that the young man in a jacket and tie was much more prosperous than he really was—two unknown men followed my father down the fairground alley. They surprised him and beat him with a rock, crushing his skull and leaving him unconscious.

They took everything of value that Larry De Morier had on him, which was four dollars and a tie clip. And when he recovered, he was left with violent seizures that he would experience for the rest of his life.

Now, although the 1950s and 1960s are often viewed through fond nostalgic eyes, there are certain areas that were not as enlightened as you might think. The popular view of epilepsy was one of them. The common belief was that the disease was a side effect that resulted from years of heavy drinking. My father, whose first and only drink was a glass of champagne at his brother's wedding, was aware of this notion. He also experienced the firsthand fear on the faces of those who looked down on him when he came out of a seizure (on the rare occasions that he couldn't slip away quietly when he felt one coming on).

His obsession for the next forty years would be with hiding his epilepsy. He had worked on the assembly line at Borden Chemical for almost twenty years when he took the janitor position there, so he could easily hide in the janitor's closet when he felt a seizure coming on. He even kept his condition a secret from my mother; they had been married two months before she saw the first seizure.

My father turned down promotions and declined other job offers because the risk of exposing his illness was too high.

On November 25, 1964, a month before my second birthday, my grandfather Eddie Elbows died. My father would stop by his mother's house every day after that to check on her, never missing a single one for the next three years until she died.

Growing up, I didn't see any of this. I just saw a man who embarrassed me, a man who couldn't throw a ball or shoot a basket because he was driving railroad spikes at the age when you were supposed to learn how to do those things. I saw a man who was getting drastically older than the other fathers because the medical treatment for epilepsy in those days was a harsh drug cocktail with severe side effects (which didn't stop the seizures from coming; they only made you so stoned that you really didn't care).

In April 1976, Larry De Morier's run of luck ran out. Feeling a seizure come on, he was not able to get his janitor's closet in time and his coworkers witnessed it. He was forced into disability.

The two areas of pride for a man of that era were his ability to work and his ability to drive to work. Larry lost both of those things on the same day.

The seizures my father experienced always came in threes; if he had one, within a few hours, two more would follow.

As a teenager, I would latch onto those times when I knew that, because of the epilepsy, my father was extra short-tempered. I would purposely say or do something to set off the delicate balance of chemicals in his head and he would become angry with me. I enjoyed these times because it was safe: My father was a gentleman and was incapable of harming anyone—and even though we would be nose to nose yelling at each other, he would never touch me. I knew this. We would yell. We would hurl threats. We would say horrible things. But he never laid a hand on me.

The next day, the seizures would occur, and the day after that, my father—now with the chemicals in his head stable—would be humiliated by the things he had said to me, ashamed. He would try to apologize.

Larry De Morier was a sensitive man, but like many men of those days, he was unable to express himself. Fathers didn't tell sons they loved them back then—that was for hippies and weirdos. My father would try to joke with me, try to get me talking, try to tell me how sorry he was, and I—the insecure and cruel kid I was—never let him. Not one time.

On November 17, 1990, Larry De Morier died. He had six dollars in his wallet—two more than he had on that day back in 1955.

Throughout my life, I was embarrassed by my father, who didn't own a pair of blue jeans or sneakers and whose favorite color was polyester. I was embarrassed by how fast he was aging, that he knew nothing of sports or the outdoors. I was embarrassed because he rode an old bicycle instead of driving a car, and I feared those times during school plays when the crowd would suddenly start mumbling and moving and I knew that out there in the dark area below the stage, my dad was having a seizure and people were trying to help him to his feet.

Who was I to be embarrassed by such a man? Who was I to look down on anyone who took such good care of all those around him, no matter what? A man who never complained. A man who never called "foul." A janitor who kept us fed and safe, whose Bible was dog-eared with use, who never had a regret, and who was grateful for everything he had.

In the years since my father died, I've managed to forgive myself for the way I treated him. I've also realized how truly lucky I was.

Larry De Morier was a much better father than I was a son. He was a gentle, loving, unselfish man. And my goal is to be half as protective and giving as a father to my own children as he was to me.

I now get it.

How to Pack a Suitcase

I love the type of movie where there is a tortured soul, filled with wanderlust, who hears the call of the open road and decides to see the world. He throws a few meager possessions in a small backpack and starts walking. He hitchhikes, he takes the bus, and he meets people along the way.

Then we get to scene five. This will be after he arrives in a town—usually to help a rancher or struggling nonprofit group out of a crisis—and he meets the girl. Scene five will be their first date. You know the scene—the darkened restaurant, the candlelit tables, he's in a suit and she's in a dress, and as you watch, only one thought goes through your head:

Really? You packed a suit in that small backpack? C'mon.

This kid has a daypack that is half-full. He carries it from New York City to Provo, Utah, and during that time he has six full changes of clothes, a suit, a raincoat, hiking boots, and sneakers, and, during the date scene, he is wearing an expensive pair of Italian loafers.

No. You did not get all of that into your twelve-pound pack.

But that's what we want. We want a bag to be light and small, yet we want it to contain a never-ending supply of clothes, coats, shoes, formal wear, and a few books—just in case we get bored. We want it to be our house—in a bag.

Types of Travel

There are two basic types of travel packing. You are either packing for weight or you are packing for content. You can't do both.

If you are going to be in three different locations over four days, if you are going to be carrying your bag through train stations and airports, or if you'll have it on your back most of the time, then you want the bag to be the smallest and the lightest one possible.

But if you are going to just one location and then back, then you want your bag to contain everything you need—or might ever need—for a specific time period. You want maximum content in a limited space.

The Suitcase Laws

Half of everything in your bag you will use.

A quarter of everything in your bag you will not use.

And a quarter of the items that you'll end up needing—you will forget to pack.

Staging

Most of us pack this way: We open the bag and start stuffing things in. When there is no more room, we're done packing. But by staging, we can guarantee that we'll pack everything we need.

Spread out the bare minimum that you need for the trip—the absolute least amount of stuff you will need. Pretend that this is all you are allowed to take and you could survive the trip if you only had that. Now pack it. When you're done, whatever available space is left over is what you have for everything else you think you might need.

Overpacking is a common—and sometimes costly—mistake. Pack too much and your free airline carry-on could easily cost you a hundred dollars or more in fees. Remember: Laundromats exist in hotels, resorts, and in every town or city you'll be in. You can always wash clothing while you're away.

And remember: If you're going to be bringing things back—souvenirs, clothing, items purchased while away—you'll need to save space for that.

Rules of the Road

Try to bring one belt, if possible—something that can be used for both casual and dress.

Try to bring two pairs of shoes—or, if needed, the pair of shoes you're wearing, one extra pair, and a pair of sandals. No more.

Packing the Suitcase

Use the roll-up method. By taking your clothing—shirts and pants, mostly—and rolling them in a tight tube, you can make the best use of space in your bag.

Pack one pair of underware for every day you'll be away, plus one extra pair. No more. And if you go somewhere exotic and end up having explosive diarrhea, all bets are off.

Wear the same clothes on your way out as you do on your way back in. This will save you one change of clothes.

Clean out your toiletries kit before you leave—otherwise, you'll be carrying those free shampoos and conditioners you took from the last trip out and then back home again. And if you're flying, remember the TSA regulations: Liquids can only be three ounces or less—unless you are checking your bag.

Pack for the weather. The forecasts for your location could change a dozen times before you get there, but it doesn't hurt to have a rough idea of what the weather will be like so you can pack accordingly.

Fill your shoes. Pack socks and underwear in the shoes that will be in your bag. This is wasted space, so fill it up.

Fill the edges of your bag first. Again, this is where pockets of wasted space often hide, so use that area first.

Use the outside pockets for items you'll want to get to quickly: phone chargers, books, magazines, and so on—so you don't have to unzip and dig through the entire bag looking for these things.

If you're checking a bag, it's a great idea to fill your carry-on with everything you'll need to survive a few days—contact lens stuff, a change of underwear, toothbrush, and so forth. That way, if your bag gets lost, you can get by while they find your bag and get it to you.

And that's how you pack a suitcase.

Now, my wife is completely anal when it comes to packing a suitcase. A week or so before she goes anywhere, the suitcase is on the bedroom floor and she will be holding rehearsals of what is going to be taken—this shirt, these shoes and . . . no . . . THIS shirt and THESE shoes. Yes.

About a day before she leaves, when we are on the final dress rehearsal of what is actually going in the suitcase, I'll add a few things under some clothes: a spatula, the upstairs cordless phone, four cans of tuna fish. Things she may need.

So she remembers us.

The Invention of Everything

Author's Note: We received several concerned emails to 543 Magazine shortly after this piece first appeared on the site. We appreciated all of them. And to answer your question—yes. Yes, we do know that this didn't really happen, but we appreciate your concerns about accuracy. Thanks again and keep those emails coming.

The sound effect of a radio dial is heard as the radio station slowly becomes clearer . . .

ANNOUNCER: It's easy to take our modern, convenience-filled world for granted. Innovation and technology have not only changed the pace of the daily experience to one that is faster and ever interconnected, but have also taken the once-sharp edges of life and rounded them down smooth. Life today is easier than it once was, which makes it extremely convenient for us to forget that most of what we now take for granted—what is today considered the baseline of modern life—is largely thanks to a handful of visionary pioneers.

Martin Renee from Utica member station WTVI, reports:

"The problem with stories like mine," Tom Protraska says as he tears the cruller from his plate in two and then eats both pieces, first with his right hand and then with his left, "is that it—it worked so well that that nobody remembers—or even really cares about what it was like before."

Tom is a very thin man, weighing in at around one hundred fifty pounds on his six-foot frame. According to his Wikipedia page, he is seventy-nine years old—even though he tells everyone that he is five years younger. Tom is bald and has a penchant for white Oxford shirts that he wears tucked in tightly.

Tom and I met at a Utica diner, where we discussed his life after he left the world limelight. It's a relatively quiet routine for him now. His days are largely spent with his wife, Gretchen, and their pug, Max. They garden, they visit their grandchildren, and Tom gets in some fishing a few times a year.

But in 1965, Tom Protraska's life was much more chaotic. Because this is when he became a worldwide sensation by first inventing—air.

"Nobody believed it would work."

Tom signals to the waitress with his empty coffee cup. "We were all breathing hydrogen and methane back then, and we had been since the beginning. And everyone was—I don't know—okay with it, I guess. I mean, how can you miss what you didn't have, right? And yeah, the Swedes were playing around with this—this xenon mixture for years. But they could never make it work."

But Tom had an idea—more like a gnawing obsession—that there had to be a better gas for humans to breathe. So, after three years of tinkering in his home garage in Utica, Tom Protraska became the very first person, ever, to breathe in a mixture of oxygen, nitrogen, and carbon dioxide. Or, what we now commonly refer to as air.

"I just stood there for a few minutes, breathing it in and out, and I couldn't believe it."

Tom's watery eyes become youthful again as he recounts the story. "I wasn't bleeding from my ears, or throwing up, or convulsing like I always had been before, from taking in all that hydrogen and methane that we all used to breathe. I was just . . . breathing. Easily, in and out. And it was working. It was really working. And that's when I knew that I had something."

But the scientific community was skeptical.

"There were still regulations back then," Tom says as he stirs his coffee. "Nothing like there is today, but there were hoops to jump through and you really needed to get with the big boys if you wanted to get anything done on a large scale. I had no idea how to do that. So, I just made the stuff and sold it out of my house."

Word spread quickly and soon Tom Protraska was earning more money selling his product part-time than he was at his full-time job with the post office. So, he left his job to make his living by manufacturing air.

"The problem was," Tom says, folding his hands across his chest, "I never patented the stuff. So, it didn't take long for others to figure out how I did it."

And then the competition came.

By 1968, air had replaced hydrogen and methane as the global standard for human and animal breathing gas. But by then, worldwide production was at its peak and Tom's garage-based operation couldn't compete with the plummeting competitive market price.

"I had few options at that point. So, I went back to work at the post office."

Since 1985, air has fallen under the public domain and is now available for free in all but three countries. There is no longer a North American market for it.

And of the 320 million people living in the United States today, more than 200 million of them have never lived in a world that breathed anything but air—or even had to pay to breathe it.

"Ah, what can you do?" Tom looks dreamily out the diner window. "The same thing happened to Brennon."

Tom, of course, is referring to Lyle Brennon, the inventor of gravity, who, in 1957, was able to patent his famous invention—but with limited success.

"He wasn't looking at the big picture—at all," says Tom.

Maureen Brennon, Lyle's widow, spoke to me by phone from her Kings River, Virginia, home. "Lyle knew he had discovered something—something really big—with that gravity thing. But he only patented it for use in sports. He didn't see any real need for it anywhere else." Maureen sighed as she gathered her thoughts. "That was dumb."

The invention, and then worldwide use, of gravity is the key historic driver that lead to the Ground Revolution of 1958. It was the paradigm shift that allowed the world to construct, interact, and make a living on the surface, rather than the space above it.

"It changed everything," says Nelson Brille, the chief economist at the University of New Mexico.

"When gravity came along, we basically threw away the old playbook. Everything was different. And everything was now possible."

Brille estimates that if gravity were still in the hands of the private sector, the worldwide global market for it would tip three hundred trillion dollars a year.

And I sit in Charlie's Diner in Utica with Tom Protraska, we discuss the changes that he and a handful of his counterparts made to the world. I ask him if it had all been worth it.

Tom's smile is bright. "Are you kidding?" He leans across the table toward me. "Breathe. In and out."

I do.

He sits back and places his thin hands behind his head. "Well, then. You're welcome."

For Utica member station WTVI, this is Martin Renee.

How to Sharpen a Knife

On my twelfth birthday, I received my very first pocket knife. It was a gift from my father and it was amazing. It was a Boy Scout knife that had two blades, a can opener, and a screwdriver that hurt your thumbnail when you tried to open it. I can still feel the black faux-wood handle and the blade as it bit into a stick or a piece of wood.

Years later, I can only remember two gifts that my dad ever gave me—even though I'm sure there were more. One was the gray tweed overcoat he had tailored for me when I turned twenty-one, which I still have but can no longer fit into, and the other was the pocket knife I got when I turned twelve, which I no longer have, but wish that I did.

This pocket-knife tradition continued with my two sons. On each of their twelfth birthdays, they received their very first pocket knife from me. And my youngest son kept my tradition going by losing his six months later.

Pocket knives have been carried by men for a hundred years or more. However, this practice was stilted somewhat by the events of 9/11. With stricter restrictions on security and safety, knives were no longer allowed on flights and in government buildings and other institutions, so many men who normally carried a pocket knife stopped in order to be compliant with the new rules.

But there are no states that forbid pocket knives.

In fact, "knives" and "pocket knives"—a pocket knife being defined as a folding knife with a blade less than three inches long—are in two completely separate categories.

Now, you're not going to get your pocket knife on an airplane as a carry-on, but you can throw it in a bag that you're checking without any problem at all. And certain federal buildings may not allow pocket knives, but pretty much anywhere else, you're not breaking any laws by carrying one.

Pocket knives are a handy tool to have and you have a right to carry one if you wish. But like all knives, pocket knives need to be kept sharp.

There are many ways to sharpen a knife and even more new gadget-y devices for sharpening blades—the kind you can use to cut a tomato and then a nail. I've tried a few of them and I've found that there's nothing better to sharpen a knife than an old-fashioned wet stone. Here's how:

Get a whet stone. These are also called "whetstones" because the word *whet* means "to sharpen." You can get one at any hardware store, department store, or flea market.

Soak the stone. Sharpening creates heat. Too much heat created while sharpening can warp your blade. That's why you should never sharpen your knife on a grinding wheel. Also, wet stones are very porous, and in order to keep the filings that come off the blade from filling the holes of the stone, you need to create a liquid coating on the surface. You can do this by soaking the stone in water for twenty minutes, or you can use mineral oil.

Identify the bevel angle. This sounds more complicated than it really is, but all it means is that most knives are beveled either below thirty degrees, or above it. Most pocket knives have a thirty-degree bevel angle, whereas kitchen knives and others are usually less. So, you want to match the angle of the blade at which the angle you are lifting the knife to sharpen it. You want to sharpen the very end of the knife, not grind down the steel around it.

Sharpen one side of the knife at a time. Position the knife at the bevel angle and pull the blade back; glide the knife along the stone gently, slowly pulling the blade back against the stone. Sweep the knife down and off the end of the whetstone. Repeat about a dozen times or so.

Repeat on the other side.

Test the blade. You can do this by slicing through a sheet of paper—a sharp blade should glide right through. Or run it rough side along your thumb—NOT blade side down. Holding the blade horizontally, run the blade across your thumb. The rougher the blade feels against your thumb, the sharper it is going across.

And that's how you sharpen a knife. It's pretty easy. And once you master it, you can show others. In fact, if you want to create a quick crowd around you during that next fancy cocktail party you're invited to, just bring up the subject of knife sharpening and watch the crowd form.

At least, I'm guessing that's how that works. Because I've never been to a fancy cocktail party. And I'm actually wondering if anyone has. Ever.

The Unexpected

On January 9, 2011—the day the Philadelphia Eagles were scheduled to beat the Green Bay Packers and move up in the NFL playoffs—I burned our house down.

It was an accident. A stupid mistake. But it was my accident. It was my stupid mistake, and because of it, our home was destroyed, our family was displaced, and our world changed.

The day before the fire, a friend had given us a goose and I smoked it along with a ham in our backyard smoker. At four that afternoon, I had taken the ham and goose off the smoker and set the charcoal pan on the cement patio to cool. Because it was twenty degrees that night, I simply poured the water tray over the charcoal instead of dousing it like I normally did.

The next afternoon—almost twenty hours later—I went to clean up the smoker and took the charcoal pan—which had stayed out all night, was cold to the touch, and even had a thick coat of ice on top of it—and dumped it in our outside garbage can. A few hours after that, some hidden spark that was still alive somewhere in the center of the charcoal pile reignited and the garbage can caught on fire. Next to the garbage can was a recycling bin full of newspapers and junk mail. That caught fire, too. Then the garage wall went up. Then the roof. Within twenty minutes, the fire had shot through the house at record speed.

The rest of the day was pretty action-packed. It included my thirteen-year-old son getting his mother out of the house safely—my wife was on the treadmill in the basement with her iPod on and couldn't hear the smoke alarms—as well as neighbors running into the burning house to help. Because I had taken my oldest son and his friends to the mall, I received one of those phone calls you hope you never get: the kind that tells you your children are hurt, your wife is hurt, or your house is on fire.

And on that day, our lives changed.

The key to this change is in the word *unexpected*. A fire is unexpected. So is a flood, a car accident, an injury at work, or a sudden death. These are all unexpected. They are events where, in the course of a single day, life tilts. It changes. These are days when you go to bed living in one life and go to bed the next night living in another. And we do this without the luxury of being able to think, *Yup, tomorrow is the day of the car accident,* or *Tomorrow is the day we'll get hurt,* or *Tomorrow is the day someone breaks into our house.* Nope. These events occur without our knowledge or permission.

And when they do, they divide time. There is the time before the fire. And there is the time after the fire. There is that world before the car accident—before you needed to learn to walk again—and there is that new world that remains afterward. There is now a dividing line that will determine the rest of your life.

Regardless of the challenges any of us have been through, we all still go through life with a protective belief that although bad things happen—and we all acknowledge that they do—they just don't happen to us. Not the big stuff, anyway. We calculate the odds and accept that these odds are basically in our favor, that the chances of one of those life-changing catastrophes happening to us are fairly slim. Sure, a layoff can happen, but not a fire. Yeah, we could get into financial trouble, but a sudden death won't happen. Our home won't be robbed. Those kind of incidents and accidents are TV plots. They're the bad things that fall into other people's lives. Not ours.

In the United States alone, there are more than three thousand house fires every day. On that same day, there will be sixty thousand injuries from car accidents and four thousand people injured while their homes are robbed. According to the U.S. Census, nine million people a year will experience one of these unexpected and life-changing events, and those nine million catastrophes will all have one thing in common: The day before they occurred, everyone involved—every single one—would have bet you their car that it wouldn't happen to them.

Now, before you label this article as one that is selling fear and roll your eyes in disgust, wait. This is not meant to shock you or shame you or compel you to dedicate four hours a week to home fire drills and weekly tire-pressure checks. The unexpected cannot be planned for, and it shouldn't be.

Yes, you can make sure your smoke alarms work and you can avoid keeping oily rags in the garage. Yes, you should have safe tires on your car and wear your seat belt. Yup. And once you have done these things, leave it alone. Because you cannot plan for the unexpected and you shouldn't waste your time worrying about what possibly might happen. You should take precautions and then you should leave it alone and live your life.

And actually, the odds are in your favor that that one of these big unexpected events won't occur to you. Out of the more than three hundred million people in this country, only nine million will experience the unexpected this year— fire, serious car accident, unexpected death, robbery, and so on. That's less than three percent.

The point of all of this is that I can now say that our fire was a defining moment for us. Now, granted, no one got hurt in our fire, so I'm cheating a little, and the things that we lost—well, things can be replaced, and they were. But during the seven months it took to rebuild our home, we had a rental house by the lake. We were unplugged from our routines and the outside world. We relied on each other and we spent more time together than we ever had before. We were closer. We were stronger.

One thing to realize is that the unexpected—those events that cannot be planned for—do happen. They occur without our consent and regardless of how prepared or unprepared we might be. And when they do, they define us.

We can't change the unexpected. We have no control. But we do have control when it comes to determining how the unexpected will change us.

How to Simplify Your Digital Life

In 1883, Florence Keynes gave birth to her first child, a son she would name John, after his father. John Maynard Keynes was bright and happy and had the advantage of being raised by a prominent English family that highly valued formal education.

Now, if you've studied economics, you know the basics of Keynes's views. He would end up changing the standard economic views of the time as well alter the way we look at governmental roles. He created in-depth theories of business cycles—which would come to be called Keynesian economics—and in the 1930s, he began to seriously challenge world economic concepts. He disagreed that free markets would always provide full employment and opposed the idea of demand leading to periods of high unemployment, arguing instead that governmental regulation would need to closely monitor boom and bust cycles.

Then came World War II, and Keynes's ideas began to be adopted by the leading Western economies, which led to the creation of the World Bank, whose goal was to end extreme poverty and increase global prosperity. And even though Keynes died in 1946, he actually became even more influential after his death. Because the governments and economic systems that had adopted Keynesian practices were now booming, they were real-life success stories that supported his theories. *Time* magazine listed John Maynard Keynes as one of the top one hundred most influential people of the twentieth century.

Now, there is no doubt about the intelligence and vision of John Maynard Keynes. It's clear that he was correct in many of his theories of economics and financial projections, and that his understanding of business and world market trends was probably better than anyone's ever. But there was one area that Keynes was incorrect about.

In fact, he was dead wrong.

Keynes began to map the growth of technology in the 1930s. He saw that the rate of development of useful tools and innovations would eventually affect society as a whole. He factored in the advances he was seeing in communications, manufacturing, transportation, all areas, across all industries, and in an essay entitled "Economic Possibilities for Our Grandchildren," Keynes made a statement that would be tied to his name from that moment on.

Keynes believed that by the time his grandchildren were adults, they'd be working a fifteen-hour week.

Technology would free us. New machinery and modernization would be the tools to take on most of the burden of our work.

Keynes stated that over time, with the help of machines, technology, and new concepts, people would become more productive.

And Keynes was—so wrong.

Well, that's not entirely true. He was right about the development of technology.

Since his death in 1946, mechanical and computer innovation has changed every aspect of our lives. We can now send information around the globe, in seconds. We can communicate with anyone we want to in written, video, or auditory format. We have access to information on any possible subject instantaneously and we can bounce signals off satellites to track our location and get us where we need to go faster and more efficiently. We can sort, organize, or trend data. And we have successfully made the world a much smaller place by opening access to every part of it.

But Keynes was wrong about how this would affect us. It didn't free us. Not at all. It only raised the bar.

If the average American needs to work forty-seven hours per week today in order to produce as much as someone did who was working forty hours a week in 1950, then that means an individual with email, spreadsheets, and a cell phone needs to work more than the same person with 1950 typewriters, carbon paper, and messenger services did. If the trend continues, we will need to increase our work by one hundred twenty percent in the next fifty years to capture the same current production rate that we have now. So, we will need to work fifteen hours more each week in fifty years, just to be as productive as we are today.

The technology that is available now is not creating less work. It's creating more, by constantly raising the competitive need—the bar that competing companies, industries and organizations are reaching. We end up doing more because we need to do more to stay in the game.

And not only has technology raised the minimum standard of work production, but it has completely altered how we think and react. We need to be wired, to be connected—all the time. If we hear that ding or buzz of our phone, we have a Pavlovian need to see what it is—no matter what we are doing or where we are.

And here is some trivia:

We are more likely to misplace our car keys than we are our cell phones, because we are, on average, away from our phones less often.

There are signs on some rural roads to inform drivers of limited cell phone coverage to prepare them for the time their phones will not work.

Phones, tablets, smart watches, and whatever is next in the technology line have all become deeply embedded in our lives. But how do we use these tools as tools and not leashes? How do we take back our lives and unhook the electronic collars?

Well, there are a few ways:

When is it ego and when is it priority? Yes, there are times when that phone needs to be glued to your hand—if you're on call, working out a customer emergency, or if someone in your family is ill. Yes, those are times when you need to work the phone. But those times are rare. Most of the time when we respond to an email during dinner, is it so we can be the first one on the email chain to do it: to save our place, to let our customers, coworkers, or the guys on the Little League committee know that we are on top of things. And that is just ego.

Respond with data. Anytime you send a work email, text, or voicemail without adding new information, you are wasting time, especially on those long email chains where the whole world is being copied. Determine what the goal is and work toward that.

Batch tasks. The most productive people out there batch their electronic chores. They answer the bulk of emails at a specific time: in the morning or late afternoon, for example. They respond to texts at lunch and return voicemails only in the car. They get more done in a shorter period of time and actually get real work done, in the real world, offline, with real people, face-to-face.

Turn off notifications. Just because your aunt posted a video on Facebook or your neighbor put her goulash recipe on Pinterest doesn't make it news. Those notifications are only distractions. Turn them off and look at them later.

Leave the phone in the car. If you look at an organization's highest-ranking individuals, they almost never arrive at a meeting, presentation, lunch, or discussion with their cell phone. They almost always leave the phone in the car. These are the people who want to be focused and want you to know that they are focused.

The simple rule is this: You wouldn't walk around all day with your hammer or a spatula. You use these things only when you need them and then you put them away. The same should be true for your phone, tablet, smart watch, or whatever other magical electronic gadget you have. Use the tool and master it. And then put it away.

You find confidence when you can distance yourself from your phone until you really need it.

John Maynard Keynes was wrong. We do not live in a world with the fifteen-hour work week. But he was right about one thing. Technology can free us. If we allow it to.

The Files

When we are born, when we first take delivery of our body, there is some setup and installation time required for the most important component we receive: the brain. Because the brain will not be operating at full power, for the first three years of life—as our brain goes through this construction and setup phase—we remain in in a state of "loading." During this period, software is installing, hardware is being assembled, code is being added in, and miles and miles of connections and cables are being strung. It's a capital project, and after several years, we are ready for some trial runs as we put our brain through its paces.

This is why any long-term memories we have tend to begin at around age three. Before this, our brain is unable to store and record. But from that point on, we are given the keys to our mind and we start to determine who we and the people around us are. What will we believe? Who will we trust? What's important, and what is our place in the universe?

In most states we're considered an adult at age eighteen, we can drink at twenty-one, we can drive at around sixteen, but we become responsible for our own thoughts at around age three.

Now, when we first start using this brand-new brain of ours, it begins in vacuum-cleaner mode as we suck up information on everything that's going on around us. Everything. Pure data. Pure experience. It's all recorded.

Then, after a few years of doing this, the brain has absorbed enough information to begin to sort through it all.

The first category we create is "Things That Are Safe," and the second is "Things That Are Scary." Everything new goes into one of these two boxes.

Once those files are established, old data are pulled out and resorted: *The chair is safe, but the cat hissed at us once, so he goes in the scary box.* For years, the world is divided into two parts: the safe and the frightening. Safe is good. Scary is bad.

Over time, we add new information and new categories: *what tastes good and what does not; what is easy and what is hard; what gets us attention and what gets us ignored.* File after file after file is filled. And we call this "personality": how we react to things, what we avoid, and what we gravitate to.

These things are what people remember about us, the footprint we leave in a crowd.

Okay, so here's the scenario:

You are now an adult, with your seasoned, battle-tested brain. And for this illustration, let's put you in prison—sorry, you've led a very troubled life.

So, you're in prison, but because you are an extremely smart convict, one day you escape. You get out of your cell, you get outside the pod, and then you make it out of the building. You climb over the wall and flee into the woods. Now, because you are a very detail-oriented person, you manage to ditch the orange prison jumpsuit and find some street clothes. You get a little cash and are a few hundred miles away before the guards even know you're gone.

Like I said, you are very, very smart.

Because you are a disciplined person, once you're free, you do not make contact with your sister in Albany or your childhood friend in Tulsa. You don't even go to your father's funeral six months later. You cut all ties with your past at places where they may be looking for you. You get a new identity, a new life, and a new job.

So, here is the question: Will you get caught?

Answer: Yes.

Why? Because without even realizing it, you will begin operating according to those old files you've created in your brain, and if the police are looking for you, they will eventually find you. And when they do, you will be making a living as a mechanic, just like you did before. You'll be on a dart league, like you were before. And you will be a member of the Moose Club and you will order rose bulbs from a catalog and drink Mountain Dew and follow the New York Giants—all like you did before. And even though your name is now Kevin Loomis, you're still the same person as before, and if the police follow your profile, they will find you and they will drag your sorry backside back to A-block.

Why? Because as disciplined as you are, you never changed your profile. You operated only according to the old files.

Now, is this programming our personality? Well, if it is, then you need to alter it or you're going back to prison. But let's leave the prison scenario aside and go deeper. What if our personality is stopping us from taking better care of our families or making more money? What if it's stopping us from obtaining a more personal relationship with God or just plain being happier? After all, this personality of ours didn't come in a box. We built it with the brain we were given. It was whittled and formed by each experience and fear and belief and desire—a trillion tiny thoughts, a million tiny events were chipped away and made us, us.

We take the same route home from work each day. We sit in the same seat during lunch. We go to the same garage when our car doesn't work, and we order the same pizza on Saturday night. Is that our personality? Is that what makes us, us? Pizza and car repair?

What's the moral of all this?

It's this:

You are not what you drive or what you eat or the team you root for. You are not even how you have chosen to act for the past thirty or fifty or seventy years. The real you—and you may not even know who that really is yet—is much, much more.

And it's your job to find out who that is. And then, once you know, dump the files you don't like or need.

And fill up some new ones.

Skill #12:

How to Clean a Fish

The Colonel—his real name is Frank, but we all know him as the Colonel—just sold his house. He lived across the street from us up until this year, when he turned ninety-eight years old and finally had to give in to an assisted living arrangement.

No one ever explained to him how a ninety-eight-year-old man is supposed to act, so you can't blame him for his ignorance. Frank is healthy, active, sharp as a tack, and lived alone in the same house he had owned since he and his late wife bought it back in the 1970s—well, that is to say he lived alone on those rare occasions when he was actually at home. Because even when he's home—that is, when he's in town—he's rarely at his house. Frank hates staying home and when he isn't on one of his trips to Maine or Florida, he'll pull out of the garage early in the morning, wave good-bye to us, pick up his sixty-year-old girlfriend, and head out for the day. I would say in any given year, Frank only spends possibly four, maybe five, months in town.

It's a depressing fact that the Colonel has a far more active social life than anyone else on our street, bar none. And most of us are four or five decades younger than he is.

Now, Frank is known as the Colonel because that's simply what he is: a retired World War II air-force colonel.

But we only give him this title behind his back. If you do slip up and refer to him as Colonel to his face, he will quickly correct you.

"Please," he'll say with a smile. "Just call me Frank."

Frank drives his own car. He plays golf—he actually participates in several senior golf tournaments every year. He competes in poker tournaments and he shoots skeet. But Frank's true passion, what the Colonel truly enjoys more than anything, is fly fishing. Frank goes on several major fly-fishing trips every year. For weeks at a time, he will fly to Maine or New Hampshire or Alaska and meet a friend or one of his sons and go fly fishing.

Trout and salmon fear the Colonel.

Now, fly fishing is a gentleman's sport and is somewhat different from the hook-and-line variety of fishing that the majority of us barbarians practice. There is an art to fly fishing, a grace that is missing in conventional fishing.

Once, I asked Frank if he kept the fish he caught.

"Naw," Frank told me. "I just like giving them a sore mouth and sending them on their way."

But occasionally, if there's a large group of people fishing with him that needs to be fed, the Colonel will end up eating a few of the salmon or trout he catches.

Even if you fish only occasionally or even once in a great while, there will come a time when you will want to keep a few of the fish you catch. And when I say keep, I mean eat. And then you'll need to know how to gut a fish.

First, go outdoors. Cleaning fish is messy business, so it's best done outdoors, preferably somewhere with water available. A makeshift table—even if it's just a piece of wood set up between two sawhorses—with a nearby garden hose works well.

Scale the fish. Hold the fish by the head and with the back end of a knife, the dull end—you can also use a butter knife or a spoon—scrape against the scales to remove them. You want your strokes to be smooth and even; otherwise, you'll cut into the meat of the fish.

Rinse the fish. This is also a good time to make sure that all the scales are off.

Cut open the fish. Holding the fish belly up, make a clean cut from the bottom of the mouth to just below the tail.

Open the fish and remove the entrails. This is the messiest part of the process, but it doesn't last long. Simply pull everything out and then cut away anything remaining. When you think you're done, rinse off the fish.

Remove the head. Depending on the type of fish you caught as well as the type of cooking you'll be doing, you can remove the head. If you're cooking over a campfire, it might make sense to leave the fish's head on. A simple stick placed through the inside and mouth of the fish will make it easy to smoke the day's catch over a fire. Also, trout cooks well with the head left on—and the scales left on, too (if cooked correctly, they will peel right off after being cooked). For pan fish—crappie, sunfish, bluegill, and so forth—or anything deep-fried, you'll want the heads and tails off.

A new family bought the Colonel's house. We watched the trucks pull up and them move in. We haven't met them yet; we'll let them get settled in. And then we'll go over and introduce ourselves. And then it will be their house.

But until we do that, it's still the Colonel's.

It's still Frank's.

The Country Club

"There you go, sir."

It wasn't the *sir* the bartender used that threw me. People call me "sir" all the time, casually, without affection; in fact, they call every male "sir" from McDonald's to Starbucks. *Thank you, sir. Here's your change, sir. Have a good day, sir.*

It wasn't the *sir*—not at all; I don't even hear that any longer. It was that, after saying it, she waited for my answer. She just stood there and waited.

The bar was busy, but not the way a commercial bar would have been. It was busy like a country club bar is— which is exactly what it was. There weren't people leaning over the wooden top, waving paper money in order to grab a Budweiser longneck and head back to the pool table. No. These were country club people. Successful people. Not only that, but Southern, country club, successful people— so it was different. It was patient and elegant and relaxed.

And hey, I'm not a total buffoon when it comes to this stuff. I've been to some elite places in my life—five-star restaurants, exclusive resorts, yacht clubs, executive ranches, mountain retreats, country clubs—none of which I paid for, or could have paid for myself, of course. That's not the point. All of them were work venues. All business trips. I've gone to a lot of places. But not on my own.

I'm grateful to have had the opportunity to see the places I have, but it means that I've been there and my family has not. In fact, outside of our one and only trip to Key West when we were first married, my wife and I have never been on a flight together. Ever. I have not been on one with the kids, either. Oh, we've taken countless car trips—too many to count—but never a flight.

I've been to Iceland, San Francisco, Luxembourg, all through Canada, the Bahamas, Las Vegas, thirty-nine of the lower forty-eight states. All for business. All without my family.

"Can I get you anything else, sir?"

And that was the question. And that's when she waited for my answer.

There were a few of us there that night who were not club members; we had come to the office for a few days of meetings and one of the owners of our company, Paul, wanted to take us all out to dinner. Just something casual. Just a quick meal at the club.

Now, it's important to note that there is nothing pompous or arrogant about Paul—there usually isn't about self-made men. He is a kind person who became very successful through hard work and smart, solid business decisions, and I have nothing but respect for him. But there is always a mental switch that gets flipped—whether by ego or fear—when you step into another man's life and take a look around. Especially when it's a successful man. The yardstick is out and the self-examination has begun.

Chris—Paul's son—was sitting at the bar laughing. Chris is one of the directors of our company, and no, he was not given that position by birthright; he earned it in every respect. He is young—somewhere in the late twenties to early thirties—sharp, hardworking, and he grew up coming to this very country club. Chris was reluctant to come to dinner tonight because he had a complete day of presentations to orchestrate for the next day and then he was taking Friday off to fly to Miami with a young lady for the weekend—just shooting down to Miami for a few days. The same way that I would just *shoot over* to Walmart or, maybe, on a whim, jet to the park with my son Alex and pitch some horseshoes.

Will my sons, Nick and Alex, ever sit at a country club like this and wonder if they have time to get back to their condo on the James River and pack before a quick weekend away in the sun? At lunch, will they compare the best fly-fishing guides in Mexico and talk about why the Oktoberfest in Munich is so much better than the one in Belgium?

Probably not.

That life is as foreign to them as it is to me. But what disadvantages do they face because of that? How many steps back on the game board have I started them out because I haven't provided that kind of life? What if I had worked harder? If I were smarter? Could I have gotten them here? Could I have gotten all of us here? And how much happier would we all be?

But then . . .

Would I want this for them, or would I want it more for the ego boost of being able to provide it for them?

And this—this type of thinking—is exactly what happens when you start to compare lives. We feel successful when we learn that a high school rival hasn't worked in three years, but we feel lazy when another one just sold his company to Google.

So, when is it okay? As a father, as a husband, as a man, when is the right time to take enjoyment in what we've provided for our families and say, *Yeah, that was enough?* When is it okay not to be complacent but to be grateful? Not to label or measure life by points but to shrug off the ego and just . . . enjoy it?

Is this something you do only when you are eighty-one years old? Is it lazy to do it when you're only in your fifties like I am?

"Can I get you anything else, sir?"

And although there were other customers at the bar she needed to get to, the bartender just stood there, smiling at me and waiting. She would not go away. She would not release me if there was anything else I needed. The others could wait. If I wanted a guitar string or a car battery or the lyrics to a Beatles song, she would get it for me before moving on to the next customer.

She just waited.

"Well," I said, smiling. "I'll let you know."

How to Remove a Tick

My son Alex is a bona fide tick magnet.

I've never seen anything like it. This kid excretes some sort of tick pheromone, a disco ball for parasites, because he doesn't only come out with new colonies of ticks that are settling in and designing a city center when we venture out into the woods; no, no, he often gets a few hitchhikers even if he just walks across a lawn or the grassy part of a parking lot—those places where the outlying ticks are, the ones that have been banned from the forests. When they see Alex coming, they sing songs and hold each other as they wait for their salvation to arrive.

In fact, when Alex, our dog Riley, and I are all in the woods together, Alex is the one will come out with ticks. When it's just Riley and me, Riley will. So, according to this highly scientific evidence, if given the chance, ticks prefer to risk the larger target of Alex—even though their chance of success is far less—than shoot for the shorter and easier one of Riley the dog.

A tick is a type of mite that falls into the external parasites category. Ticks attach to animals—mammals and birds, mostly—but they'll go after reptiles and amphibians as well. And they live off the host's blood. They burrow their mouths under the skin and start drinking.

Now, the challenge with ticks is that, unlike mosquitoes, which take a big drink and then leave, ticks are in it for the long haul. Once they have found the Promised Land, they have their mail forwarded and take up residency. And the longer they stay, the fatter they get off the host's stolen blood—and the harder they are to get rid of.

The most common ticks in North America are deer ticks and the dog tick—and they look very much alike.

Besides being unwanted, ugly, thieves, and just plain gross, ticks also tend to carry disease. Common tick-borne illnesses include Colorado tick fever, Rocky Mountain spotted fever, and of course, Lyme disease. But if you've come out of the woods with a few ticks, don't automatically think you've been exposed. Even though only a few types of ticks are capable of spreading the diseases, whether or not a person gets infected depends upon many factors, including the geographical location, the season, the type of tick, and how long the tick was attached.

In fact, even if a tick that carries a disease has attached to you, and even if it has fed on your blood, the chances of infection are still very low. For example, the deer tick that transmits Lyme disease must feed for more than forty-eight to seventy-two hours before it can pass on the disease, and most ticks are found and removed within a few hours.

But let's say you're an overly cautious individual and want to make sure that no disease was transmitted from a tick bite. Can you get a blood test to determine this? Nope. Even if you were infected, the signs of the disease in your blood won't show up for two to six weeks after transmission. But don't worry too much. As long as you catch that tick before it's been on you for three days, the odds are high that no disease has been passed.

How do you keep ticks away? Is a good offense a strong defense? Yes. And the best defense against ticks comes through your clothing. Commercial bug spray can help, but the best tick defense is to use a permethrin-based product that you apply to your clothes. Permethrin is a synthetic chemical found in insect repellent. There are many tick repellents made with permethrin, but the best one I've found is made by a company called Sawyer that carries a Duranon Permethrin spray designed for the deep woods. This stuff is amazing. I've been in the woods and watched ticks crawl on my clothes and die before they even got to my skin.

But let's say your defenses fail and you *do* pick up a tick. How do you remove it? First, here's what not to do.

When I was a kid, there were dozens of folk treatments that were used to remove ticks—many of which, we know now, you should *not* do.

The most common one was to irritate the tick to try to get it to remove itself. You could do this by lighting a match, blowing it out, and holding the hot match head behind the tick. Or you could put fingernail polish, kerosene, Vaseline, or dish soap on the end of the tick. The idea was that the tick would pull out of the skin to get away from the heat or the chemical burn.

Don't do these things.

Yes, it's possible that the tick might actually pull out of the skin. Maybe. But in panic, the tick is more likely to inject its bodily fluids before escaping—fluids that would include any disease it might be carrying. And that would be a bad thing.

The best way to get rid of a tick is the tried-and-true tweezer method. This is why it's great to carry a small first-aid kit or forty-eight-hour kit with you when you spend time in the woods. You can easily make one from an Altoids tin and keep it in your pocket.

Here's how the tweezer method works:

With a pair of tweezers, grab hold of the tick as close to your skin and its mouth as you can get.

Pull slowly back, using steady and even pressure—don't twist. And don't squeeze the tick's body, as this can send the fluids into the skin.

If the whole tick came out, great. If not, leave the part that is still in the skin alone. If you try to go after that part, you could irritate the skin even more and possibly cause an infection. Your body will eventually reject it.

Clean and treat the area.

And that's how you remove a tick.

And in case you were wondering, no. There is no cure for Alex the tick magnet.

It's a curse that he will carry most likely for the rest of his life. And one day, when he is the first man to step foot on Mars, his fellow astronaut will plant the American flag into the Martian soil and then turn to look at Alex and say,

"Holy cow, is that a tick on you?"

The Barkers

In the days before the Internet—this is when the Earth was still cooling and bread cost a nickel—telephone poles near intersections and on busy streets were often covered with rusting thumb tacks and the gummy residue of old tape. Why? Because this was where people passed by regularly, which meant that this was an ideal area to spread information to the public.

These poles became the holders of cheaply made signs for garage bands, bake sales, and fundraisers, along with desperate pleas to find lost pets. Some poles held only a poster or two, but the prime locations would be so covered with old staples and nails that the surfaces were more metal than wood. These were the go-to spots for grassroots marketing—when you didn't have a budget, when you just needed to get information out to a select group of people quickly and without cost.

Now, there was no way to track how successful this method actually was—few people who held garage sales passed out "How did you hear about us?" surveys. But the poster-on-a-pole system was easy, it was free, and it was what everybody else was doing.

Occasionally, you will see telephone poles being used this way today, but the practice is somewhat rare. You're more likely to see signs in the grassy spots near stoplights offering to get you out of debt quickly or buy that old unwanted house, but that's not the same. The garage band and yard sale advertisements have now moved to social media.

Social media sites have become the telephone pole of the Internet—a way to get the word out about your stand-up routine at an open-mic night, or when the Little League is having a car wash. Why? Because it's simple, it's free, and it's what everybody else is doing.

Now, all of us eventually will need to do some kind of promotion—whether it's to get the word out about the church's Easter play or to help increase membership in the dart league. At some time in our lives, we all need to promote . . . something. And it's very easy to think, "Hey, I am never going to do this again, I just want people to know that we're having a chicken barbecue for the Lions Club, so let me put it on Facebook and be done with it."

Yup, you can do that. In fact, most people do.

But here is an example.

Next time you're on Facebook, in the search bar, type the words *writers group*. When you do, many Facebook groups will pop up—some will be from your region, but others will be large, countrywide groups. Some of these will be massive groups of fifty thousand members or more.

If you go to one of these groups, this is what you'll see: First will be a description for the group that will say something like "This is the Tralfaz Writers Group. We are dedicated to the craft of writing and of supporting each other to develop the skill of storytelling."

Okay, great.

Next, scroll down and look at the posts. The first one you'll find will be from a middle-aged woman showing her face and her book jacket. She will tell you that her book, *Vampire School*, is now on sale for only ninety-nine cents on Amazon. The next post will be from a young man talking about his book *Space Sylum*, and that it's free all this week with Amazon Prime. The one after that will be from a college student stating that she is willing to give away a copy of her book *Wispy Danger* to anyone willing to give her an online review.

And so on.

And so on.

And so on.

There will be no discussion of prose, or storytelling, or crafting characters. In fact, there will be no discussion of writing at all; it will simply be one message over and over, from everyone there: "Buy my book, buy my book, buy my book." And that message quickly becomes white noise.

But it actually goes beyond that because these people are trying to sell books—*to people who are also trying to sell books.* That's like going up to people at a bus stop and asking them for a ride.

So, why do writers to this?

That's easy: because it's simple, it's free, and it's what everybody else is doing.

It's like the old joke where a man sees another guy under a street light looking for his lost watch. "Where did you lose it?" the man asks.

"Oh, I lost it way over in that alley. But the light is better here."

We tend to promote the way that's easiest—even if the results will be negatively affected.

When it comes to events, the trouble with social media is that such sites are a great way to get information out quickly, but they make it more difficult to track a call to action that involves attendance.

You could have four hundred people comment on your Facebook Poetry Reading Event, but that doesn't mean that four hundred will show up, because there is no connection.

It's not a commitment; they just clicked "Going" on a Facebook page.

So, then, what's the answer?

There are four promotional methods that work every time.

Don't Publicize—Promote

There are very few things in life that will make you react *just because you know about them.* We don't hear about a new movie coming out and suddenly want to see it: "Oh, *there's a new movie? Let's go.*"

No, we need more information: What's the movie about? Who is in it? What type of film is it?

The same is true for grassroots events. If there is a yard sale this Saturday, so what? There is a yard sale somewhere every Saturday. We need to know more: How big is the yard sale? How nearby? How rare are the items? What does this yard sale have that the one closer to my house doesn't?

Now, that's a yard sale. But what about other events? What if there is an opera coming to town? So what? I know nothing about opera and have never been to one—and am probably a little intimidated by them—so hearing about an opera would have no effect on me.

However, if a friend had tickets to the opera and asked me to go along, I might do it. If there were a promotion for people who had never been to the opera, giving a reduced-price ticket, maybe I'd try it. If the opera company approached my employer and offered a special rate for us, I might go. If a radio station gave me tickets and then was going to interview me right after and ask what my first experience with opera was like, yeah. Or if I knew more about the opera itself—if, by going, I felt connected to something—then yeah, I might go.

The question is: How do you get people to feel connected to it? That's the key. Is it through the idea that it's in your community? Through people you know? Through a group you support? Or just out of curiosity? You need to find that connection.

Having a community theater event? Give away tickets on a radio station or raffle them off for charity. Having a charity event? Invite a community band, local civic leader, or celebrity to be the host.

Nose-to-Nose

There was an old phrase in business back when I started thirty years ago. It said: *A face-to-face meeting is much better than a phone call.* That rule has changed. It's now: *A phone call is much better than an email.*

We are getting further and further away from our customers. Which means that those marketers who do make a direct connection have a clear advantage.

Here's an example: How many times have you seen kids outside of Walmart asking for money for their Little League or town basketball team? All the time. Those fundraisers have a low cost and bring in a lot of needed money for the group.

But how many times have those kids or parents *asked you to come watch a game?*

Probably never. They most likely just thank you for your donation and move on to capture the next person leaving the Walmart. They have a great opportunity to market directly to you—to tell you about their organization and get you involved—and yet they pass it by.

Even if they invite you and you never go, you now feel connected to them, simply because you were asked. Simply because you were included. And that links you to the event—whether you like it or not.

Show up at your neighbors' house with two tickets to that community theater event and invite them to ride with you. Go to the mayor's office with a flyer already made up announcing that he/she will be the host at the charity event.

Create an Event to Promote the Event

As much as the word *stunt* can has a negative connotation, standout events do work. Walk down Broadway in New York anytime and see how many actors in full costumes hand you a flyer and ask you to come see them later in their show.

At the Sundance Film Festival, there is a VIP and celebrity shuttling service that actually creates an event in the vehicle on the way to the film. These events are sponsored by various companies, so on the way to the film, there might be truth-or-dare questions and the winners will be given Ray-Ban sunglasses as prizes.

Why does it work? Because people want to experience new things; they want to see something cool and tell people about it.

Don't believe me? Watch the Macy's parade next Thanksgiving. This event has taken the idea to the extreme— in fact, the parade itself has become a very small portion of the program. The bulk is dedicated to the promotion of the latest Broadway shows and singers' new albums. It's presented as if it's all part of the parade, but in reality, the whole event is now one long infomercial.

One event that actually does a very good job with this concept is the county fair. If you go to a fair and head over to the areas where nonprofit groups have their displays, there will be interactive events, games, contests—all to tell you about what the organizations do, but also quickly getting you involved in it.

Having a community theater event? Get the actors in full costume to the mall and hand out flyers. Having a penny social? Hold an event where people try to guess how many pennies are in a jar. Having a bake sale? Create a free class where you make your favorite cookies in front of people and give them the secret recipe.

The only limit is what you are willing to do.

No matter how you decide to promote your yard sale, your band, or your community car wash, do it differently from how you've ever done it before. Different is remembered.

And different works.

Why?

Because it's smart, it's low in cost, and no one else is doing it.

How to Make Homemade Soup

The concept of soup is as old and established as the act of cooking itself. In fact, the very first item cooked—and I'm not referring to tossing pieces of a raw buffalo or venison over a fire but the first actual *meal*—was most likely some kind of soup.

Soup dates back to primitive humans. There is evidence of soup from thousands of years ago. Long before waterproof pots were around to boil liquid in, rocks would be heated in a fire and then dropped into a hollow log, gourd, or reed basket full of water. Then meats and vegetables were added. And boom—soup.

The word *soup* comes from either the French word for "broth" or the German word for "soak"—no one is really sure. But the experts do agree that the word *restaurant* comes from another French word that originally meant "a place to buy soup."

In the hobo jungles of the 1930s, there was always a pot of soup simmering over the fire. There, the hobos could jump on and off the freight trains and add whatever they found along their travels—a few carrots, an onion, some potato—into the communal pot.

Knowing how to make homemade soup is crucial. First of all, it gives us a low-cost food source. Soup is also a great way to reuse leftovers as well as a method to stretch food further. If you hunt, soup is the perfect way to mellow the gaminess of meats. And, like all "peasant dishes"—chili, ratatouille, shepherd's pie—homemade soup is easy, hearty, fun to make, and feeds many people.

There are many methods for making homemade soup, but this is the one I've been using for years. It's simple and allows you to add or change anything along the way.

The trinity—onions, peppers, celery—goes in a pan mixed with some butter and olive oil. You want to sweat these a bit—soften them up, but not brown them.

Place the onions, peppers, and celery into a stock pot and set aside.

It's not required to use meat in soup. In fact, I often think meat takes away from the flavor of a really hearty soup. If you do not want to use meat, potato is a great substitute because it's so dense. Another great meat substitute is rutabaga. It's extremely dense and, when cooked over a long time in a soup, it softens up but still remains firm; it also gives the soup a richer flavor. Brown your chicken, pork, turkey, beef—or whatever meat or meat substitute you want to use—in a pan. Once everything is browned, place the ingredients in the stock pot.

Next you want to add in your core vegetables—carrots, green beans, peas, whatever you want. The rule is try to use fresh or frozen first, and if you can't, then use canned vegetables. I know it may seem like an extra step but it will make a difference.

Add your liquid to the stock pot, completely covering everything. There rule here is: Water is boring. You can use just about anything—beer or wine works great; so does apple or tomato juice. I even know one guy who saves the leftover coffee to use as his soup stock. And of course, you can use beef, vegetable, or chicken stock. Now, store-bought stock is okay—and I mean, just okay—but nothing beats stock made from scratch. The next time you cook a chicken or a ham, save the bone. Toss it in the freezer and make your own stock. And remember, stock can be frozen and saved and thawed out when needed.

Next, add your spices. Remember to add spice in layers, not all at once. And keep tasting until you get the flavor where you want to be.

Once everything is mixed in, let the soup simmer. How long is up to you, but the longer it simmers, the more the flavors will marry.

Soup is universal but can contain many personal touches. It can be simple or complex. Hearty or delicate. It can be anything you want it to be.

The Five Things Our Grandfathers Would Kick Our Tails for

There's an old story about two frogs. The first frog was tossed into a pot of boiling water. He screamed—and then he jumped out of the pot. He checked himself over, took a few frog breaths, and then moved on with his frog life.

But the second frog was different. He was tossed into the pot while the water was still cool. That frog swam around. He checked everything out and saw nothing to be concerned about, so he settled in. Then the burner under the pot was turned on and the water all around the frog began to heat up, but very slowly. The frog didn't seem to notice or care. Bit by bit, the water temperature increased. There were no frog screams, no frog escape attempts. The frog simply remained in the pot until the water boiled. And until . . . dead frog.

Now, this phenomenon is often referred to as creeping normalcy or a shifting baseline. It describes what happens when change occurs slowly, in small steps, over time. Because we only see parts of the change, not the total change itself, we don't react to it.

Every day, every moment, our lives are changing. What seems normal today was not normal just a few years ago.

Yes, technology has something to do with this. But the big changes, the sweeping changes, the "dead frog" changes, have very little to do with technology. These changes are driven by shifting priorities and varying acceptance.

Let's turn back the clock a bit and take a look at our normal, everyday lives through someone else's perspective. Let's go back in time, not simply to my generation—born in the 1960s—but before that—to the people born in the 1920s and 1930s. This is the generation that fought in World War II. This is the generation that fought in Korea—in fact, many World War II vets volunteered to fight again in Korea. This is the generation that was raised through the Great Depression. This is the generation that struggled and sweated and built the structure of this country and became what Tom Brokaw called "the greatest generation."

If we are going to look at the everyday structure of our society, then what better to view it through than the eyes of that group of people?

So, what would the greatest generation, our grandfathers (if you're part of my generation), think of the everyday, basic, routine aspects of our lives today?

There are five things that our grandfathers would kick out tails for.

Bottled Water

Bottled water is one of those "dead frog" changes that has built up slowly over the past few decades and is now so embedded in our culture that we don't even notice it. But think about it. We are paying for water. Yes, we technically pay for the water that comes out of the tap. But when we buy bottled water, we are paying dollars for something we already pay pennies for.

The stuff that comes out free from sinks and water fountains and garden hoses?

Water.

Which means that for bottled water, in a factory someplace, someone turns the tap on, filters the water for taste—because our sensitive, twenty-first-century palate wants all our water to taste the same—and then squirts it into plastic bottles, which we buy by the truckload.

Say we yanked a solider off the battlefield in World War II and brought him to the modern day, gave him three bucks, and said, "Okay, go to that convenience store and buy me a bottle of water."

The soldier would look at us strangely. He would walk into the store and open the cooler. He would pick up the water and look at the money you gave him and then look at the bottle of water. He would check the ingredients—nope, just water. And then he would walk back to you.

"No," he'd say. "I can't do it."

It would be so foreign to him that he wouldn't be able to do it.

The Backyard Deck

Backyard decks are great places. They're where we entertain family and friends, where we barbecue, and often where we relax. But in our grandfathers' day there was a place called the front porch and it was a social place—an open and connected place to sit and visit with neighbors.

During our grandfathers' time, it was very common to finish dinner and take a walk. And during this walk, you would stop and visit with the folks sitting on their porch. You would connect with the neighborhood, hear the gossip, and check up on people. When you had visitors at your home, you often sat on the porch. When you listened to the ball game, you did it on the front porch so anyone could stop and listen with you.

The front porch was open. The front porch was inviting.

When the front porch became merely decorative, when walking after dinner became less popular, then people in our neighborhoods became less involved with us and we became less connected to them. Now, we can now drive into our driveway, hit the electronic garage door opener, drive into the garage, and never see our neighbors.

Logos

Your grandfather probably had a set of Esso "Put a Tiger in Your Tank" coffee mugs. They were thick and white and very common, and he probably owned a few of them. Why? Because they gave them away free when you purchased Esso gas. Your grandfather had coffee cups with the Esso tiger logo on it because they were free. No other reason. If they had offered to sell those very same mugs—even at a low cost—your grandfather would have sneered.

Why would I pay to buy someone's name on a mug?

But today we do. We actually pay—and pay quite a bit—for clothing, coffee mugs, key chains, or hats that say Aeropostale, Harley Davidson, or Nike.

And I haven't even mentioned the sports logos. With sports logos, we pay for the right to promote our favorite teams. What would your grandfather say if you spent eighty bucks to wear your favorite quarterback's jersey?

Your grandfather would want to know why any man would want to put another man's name on his own back.

"What's wrong with your own name?" he'd ask. What's wrong with doing something you are proud of instead of pretending to be someone else?

Credit

Before you argue that there wasn't credit available in your grandfather's day, it's not true. Of course there was. There has always been credit, even before the rise of actual credit cards. The difference is that in your grandfather's day, credit was seen as a weakness, not a reward. In our grandfathers' day, the people who used credit were the ones who could not afford to pay in cash. They were looked down on because a man in debt was no man at all.

Credit meant bad planning. Credit meant that you didn't earn enough to take care of yourself and your family. The men who lived through the Great Depression and fought in foreign lands and came back home to raise families had only one rule: If you can't afford it—meaning you don't have the cash money to buy it—then you go without it.

T-Shirts

Yes, your grandfather owned T-shirts—he wore them under his dress shirts. And the only time you saw him in wearing only a T-shirt was when he was sitting in his chair listening to the ball game, or when he was outside mowing the lawn. If someone came to the door, he would grab his dress shirt and pull it on before answering.

When your grandfather went out to eat, he wore a tie. Even if he was a blue-collar guy, he had a sense of pride in how he looked.

Whether you were a ditch digger or a doctor, a lawyer or a shoeshine man, you took pride in your appearance.

Today, dress is casual—well, that's what we call it, but casual has fallen into a whole new category. Now, we have work clothes and everything else. We don't dress up for dinner at a restaurant, much less for dinner in our own homes.

Your grandfather did. He would often get dressed up to eat dinner with his wife and family. Because it was an event. He was proud to have earned the money to pay for the food. He was proud of his home and wife and children.

Your grandfather had pride.

And that's probably what it boils down to. Pride. Our grandfathers had it and we as modern people are lacking it.

Why did they have it? Because they deserved it. They fought and sacrificed and planned for it. They earned that pride—it wasn't given to them; they paid for it several times over.

When is the last time we sacrificed or went without? When is the last time that we felt real pride in something—not simply pride in a new car we owe money on or the comforts we can rent, but true, bone-deep pride?

For most of us, it's been a long time. And this doesn't mean that our generation is far worse than the ones before it. But it does raise an interesting question. And that is, when our grandkids talk about what we stood for, what we cared about, and what we fought for—what will that be?

Skill #478:

How to Split Wood with an Axe

For the first twelve years of my life—from 1962 until 1974—I lived in this place in Upstate New York named Sanitaria Springs. It wasn't a town—it was barely a village—but it was a great place to be a kid and an amazing place to grow up.

The town was originally named Osborne Hollow and later changed its name when, in 1892, Dr. Sylvester Kilmer wanted a location for a health sanitarium and chose the area because of its natural phosphate springs. But before he started construction, he convinced the town to change the name to Sanitaria Springs—if you were sick, would you want to go to Osborne Hollow? Kilmer's sanitarium was built, in addition to a hotel—which became the house my parents later bought and where I grew up—as well as a bottling plant and stores.

The sanitarium fell into disrepair after the death of the good doctor—who actually claimed to have taken the cure for cancer to his grave. Then the sanitarium closed but the town moved on.

By the time I came along, remnants of the old days were still there. The place where my dad dragged our garbage cans out for pickup was the old horse trough for the hotel, and at my cousin's house up the street were the original stone steps where horses and buggies would pull up to let off their passengers.

Sanitaria Springs was a place all its own. Long before the highway came in, it was rare and hidden and all ours. It was a place where fields became baseball diamonds, gravel pits became swimming holes, and barns became haunted houses.

It's just a ghost town now, just a name printed on Exit 4, off Route 88 South, and although I think the fire station is still there, as well as a few houses and a chain gas station that popped up ten years ago or so, the places I remember—Shirley's Store, the post office, the Grange, the school, my parents' fish store—are all either empty buildings or are gone completely. Some say it was the highway that killed the town. Others said it would have died anyway. It doesn't matter. What matters are the memories—and all of them are good.

I learned to do many things in Sanitaria Springs. I learned to ride a bike, pitch a tent, and how to split wood. And many of these things I learned were through my cousin Chris McAvoy.

I idolized Chris and still remember many of the things he taught me about camping and hiking and being a man. One thing Chris taught me—while we were building go-carts from flowerboxes we had stolen from our house—was how to use a hammer and how to use an axe. He taught me by telling me one rule—the same rule I later passed on to my kids.

And that rule is this:

Let the tool do the work, not you. Hold the axe low, swing, and let the weight of the axe do the job.

So how do you split wood with an axe?

Find a base to cut on. Place the wood to be chopped on a stump or block of larger wood you will use to cut on.

This is an efficient way to cut—by raising the wood you are cutting—as well as being safer, so you don't have to bring the axe down farther than necessary or damage the axe blade by digging it into dirt.

Place the wood longways up and make sure it's steady.

Take a solid stance. Place your feet at shoulder width apart.

Swing your axe around. Keep your grip on the handle midway until you bring the axe around and are starting to swing back down with it. Then move your hands to the base and bring the weight off the axe head down on the wood. This is where you're letting the axe do the work.

And that's pretty much it. Repeat this process until all the wood is chopped, or you are as muscular as the Brawny paper towel guy.

Either one is fine.

Grace

There are many words in the English language that have changed meaning over time. For example, the word *artificial* originally meant "artistic" or "crafty." The word *decimate* meant "to reduce by one-tenth," and in the original Latin, the word *nice* meant "ignorant" or "unaware."

In only the years since the nineteenth century, the meaning of the words *dinner* and *supper* have changed: Dinner used to refer to the large meal of the day—often eaten in the early afternoon—and supper meant the smaller meal eaten later at night—often after 7:00 P.M. Today, both words are interchangeable and both refer to the evening meal.

In the modern world, many other words have changed meanings. Spam, once only the name of a processed and canned meat, now refers to the mountains of junk emails we receive daily. A cursor was the word for a running messenger and now refers to the movable indicator on a computer screen. The word *friend* once applied only to those people with whom we have a close personal bond and connection but is used now for anyone who follows our Facebook or Twitter page.

In my opinion, one of the most interesting word changes involves the word *offensive* or the phrase *to offend*. These words have long been in existence—for hundreds of years—but only in the past decade or so has the meaning altered and even grown confusing.

During the Vietnam War, American television announcers warned viewers when upcoming footage from the war would be offensive—that is, when it would contain graphic images of violence. We knew what the word *offensive* meant then.

At that time, domestically, we were a country divided by race, hate, and fear. A man with dark skin had the right to fight and die as a soldier along with his white counterparts—a first in American history—but he could not attend the same church or use the same public restroom.

To say such things were offensive would be a great understated truth.

Then, in 1954, the Supreme Court case of *Brown v. Board of Education* overturned decades of segregation by race and declared that separate educational facilities for black and white students were "inherently unequal." But even with desegregation technically the law of the land, there was more violence. And more fear.

Slowly, as the decades passed, the race walls began to crumble. Slower yet, the hate and fear began to fade.

Then came September 11, 2001.

And everything changed.

Religion became the new race. We were frightened and angry and confused and we were told that a world split by religion could only be mended by understanding and tolerance. Fueled by a desire for healing, we embraced this word, *tolerance*. And there were more words that were added to our lexicon. The more words that got mixed in, the vaguer and more confusing everything became.

Instead of showing kindness, we were asked to be objective. Instead of understanding, we were encouraged to be respectful. Instead of being neighborly, we were told to be civil. And above all, the ultimate focus was to never say or do anything that might be ever be perceived as . . . offensive.

And because we never truly understood the new meaning of this word—*offensive*—we did not understand what it truly was to offend. So, we simply took the easy path and avoided any and all areas that even might offend. And that meant anything religious or spiritual.

And so, the new segregation began.

Which brings us to this, the ultimate irony and the ultimate truth.

I believe in God. I believe in a God that created me and watches over me and who is with me on Earth and will be with me in heaven. There is no need for me to apologize for this because there is nothing offensive about it.

As human beings, we need to work less on being tolerant and more on being generous.

We need to be less objective and more helpful.

And we need to be less unbiased and more forgiving.

And above all things, we need to be grateful: grateful to our God, grateful to our family and our neighbors, and grateful to all that is on loan to us for the short time we live in this world.

And during that Thanksgiving or Christmas or Easter or that visit to someone else's home, if we are extended the honor to say grace over the meal, we should embrace it.

If you've never publicly said grace over a meal, the rules are simple.

We are thanking God for the meal. We are thanking God for the chance to be at that table with family and friends. We are expressing our thanks that we live in a place where food is plentiful and we can live and work without fear or danger. We affirm that we will work hard to show love and kindness to everyone we come in contact with.

And we are grateful, in the true sense of the word: that we don't deserve the good things we have, we can't earn them, and we aren't naturally entitled to them.

But we are very glad that they are there.

How to Remove a Splinter

There is a story in my family about my great-great-grandfather—or maybe he was a great-great-uncle. It doesn't matter. So, this grandfather—or uncle—got married and lived with his wife in a cabin on a small farm. This cabin had a rough wooden floor, and if you had stocking feet—or, worse yet, bare feet—you would end up with a foot full of splinters. Every stinking time.

Now, the first few years on the farm were tough. Sometimes, the two of them barely had enough to eat, but they worked through it, and this grandfather—or uncle—and his wife had their first child. Time went by and life did not become any easier, especially now that there was another mouth to feed, until one day, after a few additional years of struggle (as well as a few more years of yanking splinters out of his feet), the grandfather-uncle finally had enough.

He went to his wife and said, "Maggie"—I'm guessing her name was Maggie because that sounds like the right kind of name—"Maggie, we're not making a go of it here. So, this is what I'm proposing. You go back to your people. I'll go back to my people. We'll leave this marriage and we'll leave this farm the same way we came into it. As separate people."

And Maggie, being a very wise woman, said, "Okay, fine. We'll leave the marriage the same way we came into it.

Which means that I came into it without a child. So, you'll be taking the boy with you."

Now, as kids, when we would hear this story, the first thing we noticed was that when the story ended, every time, all the adults laughed. Every one of them.

And we, the children of the family—possibly concerned about learning that starving was viewed as only slightly worse than parenthood—never laughed. Ever.

But the even more disturbing part of the story was that my grandfather or uncle and his wife decided to stay together because being a parent was only slightly better than a foot full of splinters. That's the part that got us kids—that with a choice, this person would be a father, only if he could avoid having his foot jabbed with pointed pieces of wood.

But the good part of the story—or what the adults said was good—was that they didn't split up. They stayed together. In fact, the two eventually made the farm work and even remained married for over forty years and—here comes the good part—they had nine more children.

All the adults always laugh at this part, too.

Us kids? Not so much.

But the mental image of this that has stayed with me all these years is the idea of a foot full of splinters.

Can you imagine a foot full of splinters? Actually, that sounds like a great country song, because the truth of it is that even a single splinter, just one, is bad.

The rule about removing splinters is simple: The bigger the splinter, the easier it is to remove. The smaller the splinter, the more it will want to hunker down and get cozy. So, let's focus on the small and nasty splinters here because the larger ones usually come out easier.

The aspect that's tricky about removing a splinter is that the splinter is often under the skin far enough where you have to dig in through the skin to get to it—the needle method—

or clip away parts of sensitive skin with nail clippers or small shears in order to get to it. This is the worst part, because you are often causing extra pain to someone who is already in pain.

But if you do this right, you can do it almost painlessly.

Now, over the years I have seen many methods of removing splinters. I've seen people use duct tape or glue. I had an aunt who was pretty good at removing them with an uncooked, sliced potato. I've seen people soak bread overnight to draw the splinter out, use egg shells, or place bacon fat over the splinter. I even knew a Little League coach who kept a cut piece of ladies stocking in the first-aid kit. He would use the stocking to snag the end of the splinters we always received from the wooden bats, enough to pull the splinter out with tweezers.

And although I've seen most of these methods work, they have not always worked for me. For me, there are only two ways to remove a splinter: the dry method and the wet method.

The Dry Method

Wash your hands, wash the area with the splinter, and wash a pair of tweezers and a pin. Now, this is easy if you're in your kitchen, but many times you get a splinter in the woods, on a camping trip, or from a canoe paddle and don't have that luxury. If you have a first-aid kit handy, use some peroxide or alcohol wet naps to clean the area of the splinter and your tweezers. Or run the end of the tweezers and pin over a flame to sterilize them. If none of these options is available, get the splinter out and then clean the area as soon as you can to avoid infection.

Feel for the end of the splinter. This is the key. A splinter can be removed easily if you can get to the end of it. If you can find the end, try to get the tweezers around it and gently pull out along the same path it went in on.

Get to the end of the splinter. If the splinter is in too deep to get a pair of tweezers around it, then you have to either get the end up with a pin or cut away the skin to reach it. This is not always as easy as it sounds, but if the area is very sensitive, you can numb it with some ice, or if you have any bee or wasp sting spray, that works well, too. Enough ice and this part will be pretty painless. The main thing is to focus and remove the splinter.

Clean the area again—or as soon as you can—to avoid infection.

The Wet Method

There are many wet methods of removing a splinter, but the one I have used on my kids involves a simple baking-soda paste—I've used this to get bee stingers out as well.

Mix baking soda and water together. You are looking for the consistency of paste.

Place the paste over the splinter and cover with a Band-Aid or with gauze and tape. Let the paste stay over the splinter for an hour or two.

Remove the gauze. More than half of the time, the splinter will have been removed. If not, you can try the dry method or . . .

You can do nothing.

Splinters want to remove themselves naturally—through our movements and the movements of the skin, they will eventually back out on their own. It's just a question of how painful the splinter is and how quickly you want it gone.

My wife, Debbie, is amazing at getting splinters out—or maybe she just enjoys poking me with a needle. She takes my hand and with her other hand she quickly finds that demon piece of wood with the needle tip, and pop, removes it. Done.

And every time she does this, every time she stops the pain, I think of that story about my grandfather, or uncle, or whoever he was. And I ask myself if I had to choose between a life with feet full of splinters, or one without her, what would I choose?

And then I think that splinters aren't so bad.

The Weight Goal Secret

It is almost impossible to turn on a television, go online, or look at a magazine or even a newspaper—remember those old things?—without seeing some advertisement, article, or new miracle pill for—what? Of course. How to put on pounds. How to get big. How to get fat and how to remain overweight.

It's everywhere—especially around the beginning of the year when our New Year's resolutions are the most powerful and we all want to get as big as we possibly can, as quickly as we can. America as a country is obsessed with the image of being overweight—the relaxed melancholy feeling that it gives you, the slow and steady shuffle it lets you move with, and the overall positive image of being fat. In fact, the entire weight-gain business is a sixty-billion-dollar industry—and that's just in the United States alone.

That's sixty *billion* dollars. Hey, Linda Moody's book and DVD series, *Fat for Life,* has sold more than two hundred million copies worldwide—not bad for a skinny kid who was able to turn her life around. And for over twenty-one years, more people have tuned in daily to *This Time, I'll Keep It on* than watch *Dr. Oz, Ellen,* and *The View* combined.

We all want to look like our favorite cooking-show hosts, bus drivers, and salesmen. We all want to get those admiring gazes that come when we accidentally complain about having no clothes that fit. We all want those extra XXs after the size on our shirts and we all want the snoring sounds we hear from the house next door to be our snoring sounds. Of course we do.

The good news is that I'm here to tell you it's really not very difficult. In fact, every weight-gain book, every personal weight-gain trainer's advice, every DVD can be boiled down to two simple rules: Eat more and move less.

That's it. It's really that easy. Everything beyond those basics is just detail.

Now, all the experts will also tell you that you need to mix in a solid, relaxed regiment of physical rest—at least twenty to thirty times a week—for true, long-term weight gain. This is true. But they will also tell you that unless you get the food aspect taken care of, the physical rest won't get you there by itself. So, in this article, I want to focus only on the food aspect of your weight-gain plan—if you're looking for great physical rest routines and suggestions, I recommend Almon Tonie's books *Avoiding Injuries* and *Ready to Sit*.

Here is the one secret strategy, the single secret, you need to help you gain weight, get fat, and this time, keep it on.

Ready? Here it is.

Food is love.

That's it. With our incredibly busy lives, it's so very easy to forget what food is. We get moving along with our day and we often just think of food as—well, just food. Nothing more. We see it as nothing more than fuel for our bodies. And when we look at food this way, it becomes no more than the gasoline we put in our cars.

And this is so, so untrue.

Food is a reward. Food is a treat, food is medication, and of course, food is love. It's how we show the people around us that we care about them. It's how we give back to coworkers. It's how we reward our children and how we demonstrate to others—as well as ourselves—that we matter and that we're important.

How many times have you been so busy that you forgot to eat? How does it make you feel when food just becomes nothing but fuel? What holes are left in your day?

To fully realize the impact of the idea that food is just fuel, take a few seconds and imagine how empty your day would be if this were true. What would you fill your time with? And what about all the time you should be spending thinking and planning what to cook and where to eat? What would take the place of all those hours? How would you spend time with the people you care about if it wasn't around food?

The answer is, you couldn't. There is no other way.

So, the next time you are eating—and experts agree that, to achieve solid weight gain, you should eat just past the point where it's painful—ask yourself: What do I get out of this particular food?

If your answer is nutrition, fuel, or energy, then you have a poor food image.

But if your answer is reward, self-medication, or a cure for boredom, then you have the solid structure you need to move forward in your weight-gain journey.

And of course, don't forget your quantities.

Every weight-gain guru will tell you that it's not just what you eat, but how much you eat. Yeah, yeah, yeah. We're all sick of hearing this because we all know that we need to eat more. But it's not always so easy.

Remember, the more you eat—the more you eat. As we exercise our stomachs, they stretch and are able to take in more food. As we train our bellies, we can take more, but remember that this takes a while—sometimes days—so don't hurt yourself.

Make today the day you begin this incredible quest.

And remember, I believe in you.

You can do this.

Skill #55:

How to Make Jerky

Tracing the history of jerky is somewhat difficult because people have been salting and drying meat for centuries. However, the word *jerky* has a direct line back to the ancient Inca, sometime around the year 1550. The Inca would cut slices of llama meat, rub it with salt, and dry it in the sun or over a fire. When the Spanish conquistadors arrived, they saw this process and called the dried meat *charqui,* and when they later invaded the Americas, they noticed that the natives were doing a similar process with meat from buffalo, deer, and elk. The Native Americans began using the same term—*charqui*—only with their accents, they pronounced it "jerky."

Jerky allowed people to produce a high-protein fuel that would be readily available and eat it when food was scarce. It became a staple food item for early American pioneers and aided in Western expansion. Over the years, people discovered that the meat could hold more flavor if certain spices and tastes were added, and they began to create jerky for flavor, not only as a survival food.

Now, as far as nutrition, beef jerky is actually a pretty healthy snack. It's a great source of protein, is low in fat and calories, and has minimal carbohydrates. Yeah, the sodium content is through the roof, but hey, it's salted meat—what do you expect?

And remember, jerky is not just a snack food. Jerky is dehydrated meat, which means it can be rehydrated again when placed in hot water, so you can use it in chili, stews, at home, or while camping or hiking.

But here's the thing. The cost of commercial jerky is downright ridiculous.

Let's use a typical bag of beef jerky as an example. The brand I found had a retail cost of around $6.00 for a 3.25-ounce bag. If we take $6.00 and divide it by 3.25, we find out that this jerky cost $1.85 an ounce. And because there are 16 ounces in a pound, that means the cost of this jerky is . . . $29.60 a pound.

That's thirty bucks a pound for beef jerky.

Just for a quick comparison: At the time of this writing, lobster is currently running around twelve dollars a pound, filet mignon is nineteen dollars a pound, and prime rib is about seventeen dollars a pound.

But beef jerky—that you buy at the gas station—is thirty dollars a pound.

Now, add to this the difference between the taste of homemade jerky and the prepackaged kind and it's not even worth comparing. The jerky you can make at home tastes worlds better, hands down, and will not contain any strange chemicals, preservatives, or nitrates.

Marketers jumped on this fact a few years ago and starting producing small commercial dehydrators to allow you to dry your meats and vegetables at home. They created infomercials, bought television time, and dominated the shopping channels, stating what a crime it was for you to pay so much for beef jerky when you can make it yourself. But they would like you to make it at home—with their two-hundred-dollar dehydrator.

That's just plain silly.

Why would you pay two hundred dollars for something that is basically a little heater and fan? And why would you pay any amount of money for a device that can do what the Inca did in the 1500s with just some fire and the sun?

Everything you need to do to dehydrate—herbs, vegetables, meats, anything—can be done in your kitchen oven.

And it doesn't matter what type of meat you use. You can use beef, venison, turkey, salmon, tuna, or something even more exotic. And you can cater each batch to different tastes—sweet, smoked, or spicy.

So how can you make your own jerky? Here's how.

Cut the meat into strips. You'll want these to be about the size of a slice of bacon. The best way I've found is to get your butcher or meat department in the supermarket to cut the meat for you.

Prepare the marinade. Here is a very simple marinade that works well:

¼ cup Worcestershire sauce
¼ cup soy sauce
1 tablespoon honey
2 teaspoons black pepper
1 teaspoon chili powder
1 teaspoon crushed red pepper flakes
1 teaspoon liquid smoke
1 slice of onion
1 squeeze of lemon

1. Place the meat in the marinade and then in a freezer bag or storage dish, cover with foil, and refrigerate anywhere from two hours to overnight.

2. Preheat the oven to 160°F.

3. Place a cookie sheet, wrapped with aluminum foil, in the bottom of the oven. This is to catch all the drippings from the jerky, because you are going to place the jerky right on the oven racks.

4. Allow the meat to dry in the oven for anywhere from six to twelve hours.

And that's it. Homemade jerky.

Now, don't forget: This stuff won't have the preservatives that the commercial kind does, so I wouldn't throw it in a bag and forget about it for a few years. But several weeks or even a month or so shouldn't change the taste. Jerky is great to keep in the car, at your desk, or on hand the next time you meet an Inca.

Rum Oatmeal Energy Bars

When I was fourteen years old and my sister was twelve, my mother went back to college full-time to get her nursing degree. Up until then, my mom had been the stay-at-home type—pretty typical of the 1970s—but when my dad was no longer able to work because of an injury, our painfully tight budget was about to get a whole lot tighter. Which meant that at the age of fifty-four, Velma De Morier set out to burn through a two-year technical nursing degree program in one year, and then go to work as a nurse.

Now, with my mother off at college all day and studying all night, my father and my sister and I had to kick in with the housework and the cooking. And because the nutritional content of my father's famous "burnt water with gray stuff" was extremely limited, I decided that this would be a good time for me to learn to cook.

One very simple dish that I got pretty good at was—well, I really don't think it had a name, but it consisted of some form of pasta, some form of frozen vegetable, a can of tuna fish, and Italian dressing. I could make this fast and easily, and it was probably the main reason the four of us survived that year.

Later on, when I was in college myself, I perfected this pasta dish so that it actually included spices—something I hadn't thought of before—and for pennies, I could make a pot of food that I could eat for days.

And then, at the end of my freshman year, I came across the ultimate recipe: Rum Oatmeal Energy Bars. And everything changed. I lived on those bars all through college and for a solid decade afterward.

It's pretty simple process to make Rum Oatmeal Energy Bars and even though I haven't made them a while, I still remember what to do.

You'll need one bottle of Captain Morgan's Spiced Rum, one cup quick-cooking oats, half a cup of dark raisins, a quarter cup whole-wheat flour, a stick of salted butter, and . . . well, some other stuff, but we'll get to that.

Now, the first crucial step—and you have to believe me on this—the absolutely *very* first step is that you have to begin by drinking one ounce of the rum. I know, I know—weird. But there is something about drinking the rum that allows you to taste-test the other ingredients. Without that first taste, the whole process doesn't really work.

So, pour the rum and drink it. Done.

Now, the second step is to arrange all your ingredients on the countertop—you'll need to be able to see everything and then go back when needed. So, get a glass baking dish and place it on the countertop next to everything else.

By the way, the countertops we use in our kitchen aren't granite countertops—which are all the rage right now. They're Corian countertops, which cost us a little less but are just as good. In fact, the guy who sold them to us—I think his name was Ken—said that the resale value of these countertops is just as high as the granite ones. Actually better.

Okay, so we spread out all our ingredients along with countertop, along with the one ounce of the rum. Now, I don't know if I told you this, but you have to drink one shot of the rum. Yeah, I know, weird. But trust me; it's the only way it works. So, pour a shot of the rum and drink it. Done.

Okay, now spread everything across the countertop. Your raisins, the flour, in fact—okay, this will be cool. Okay. Listen. Listen. Okay, take the flour and pour it in a bowl and hollow out the center of it—you know, like a mashed potato bowl before you put in the gravy? Like this, and then make little roads up the flour like this. See? See what I'm doing here? It's like a dirt-bike track. And then the bikes can climb—right up the—to the jump. See? Oh, that's so, so cool.

Okay, now the first thing to do is pour a shot of the rum and drink it. I know, I know. Shut up. Just do it. So, you pour the shot and done.

Okay, now you take the ingredients, all of them—the raisins, the cordless phone, the flour dirt-bike track, and some other stuff, and you just fan it all across the countertop. See, just fan it.

Now, these aren't the fancy granite countertops like I wanted. Nope. Not at all. My wife, Debbie, wanted to save money. So, her and that jerk Ken said, "Oh, Corian is just as good."

Yeah? Well. Bull. Who says, "Hey, come over and see my Corian countertops," huh? Who? I'll tell you who. Nobody. That's who. That's exactly who. No-frickin'-body. That's who.

So, you spread everything out over the crap, cheap, I-don't-work-hard-enough-to-afford-granite countertops and you pour yourself a shot of the rum.

Yeah, well, shut up and drink it.

Okay, now you spread everything across the countertops—make sure to cover the stains and the chips that aren't supposed to happen but always do because Ken is a liar and a loser and couldn't tell the truth if his life depended on it. And take a shot of the rum.

Don't make me come over there. Just drink it. Boom and done.

Okay now, did I ever show you my grandfather's powder horn? It's really cool and supposedly my grandfather carried it in World War I—but that doesn't make sense because they didn't use powder guns back then, so my mother probably lying to me, too. Just like Ken—the jerk.

She probably told Laura the truth about the powder horn, though. Laura—she's so perfect.

Hold on. I'll call my sister, Laura. She lives in Ohio.

Okay, I tried to call my sister but the phone is at the bottom of the flour dirt-bike track, and when the phone rings it looks so cool so I left it there.

Okay, so the first step is to take a shot of the rum.

Boom. Done. Nailed it.

Okay, now this is what we're going to do. Okay? Are you listening? Okay, here is what we're going to do. This will work. We are going to move all the ingredients over to the dining room table and work there instead. Because that's a solid wood table. Oak. Made in America. And if we move everything in there, things won't roll off the countertop because this counter was never installed properly and will most likely catch on fire. I mean it—mark my words—*this countertop will kill somebody!* It's an unholy, godless countertop installed by Nazis—I am so serious that one guy had a Nazi tattoo—he said it was a birthmark but it looked just like a swas . . . a swizzle . . . a swarmi—whatever those Nazi things are called. It looked just like it.

Okay, so we're at the dining room table now and we have everything spread out. Okay, we take a shot of the rum. Done. Okay. Okay, so—we spread it all out over the surface of the table and . . . Wait.

Now, this is a good time to eat the raisins. Raisins are good for you and besides your stomach is probably feeling a little off right now. So, eat the raisins and then do another shot of the rum.

Pow. Done.

Now, when I was in college, I had the chance to go work on a long liner—you know, one of those big fishing boat thingees? For the summer. For the entire frickin' summer. But know what? Guess what. Guess. Go ahead. Ready? I didn't go. Nope. Not me. I had no reason not to go, either. All my friends went. All of them. Buckethead, Bear, that—that other kid, I can't remember his name. But not me. Oh no, not me. I chickened out and worked in a pharmacy for the summer instead. Now that was fun. A pharmacy.

Okay, so here is what we're going to do. We're going to move all the ingredients from this fine American-made oak table to the couch because that's more comfortable and because I taped a bunch of *Lost in Space* episodes and we can watch them all in there while we cook.

Debbie picked out that couch and it's perfect for putting ingredients together on and she did a great job, didn't she? She's so good at stuff like that. She's so good at everything. Everything she does. I'm so lucky to have her. I love Debbie.

Okay, so first we need to get all this flour out of the fish tank.

When . . . ? When did we get a fish tank? Oh, wait, that's . . .

Oh, man. That's funny. That is so funny. I thought it was a fish tank but—but we don't. . . . Oh, man, that is the funniest—I actually thought . . .

Okay, so this is tickin' me off a little. What? I've got the DVR going but every time I press *Lost in Space,* an episode of *Dancing with the Stars* comes on.

Dancing with the frickin' Stars? Are you kidding me? Over *Lost in Space.* No way. No frickin' way.

Okay, so we've got *Lost in Space* going and have all the ingredients spread out under the couch cushions so the turtles won't get them. Not real turtles. Duh, I mean—I mean . . . Shoot, what's the word? Cats. Cats. Did I say turtles? Why did I say turtles? We don't have turtles.

That's funny. That's so—so funny.

Okay, so we do a shot of the rum. Pow. Done. I am the greatest.

Now, we take the other couch cushions and put them on the floor and make a little fort. This will help with the . . . Wait.

Did I tell you that my mother—my mother, at the age of seventy-nine went back to college to be a doctor to support us?

Can you believe that? At almost eighty-five frickin' years old she went back to college to support all fourteen of us kids.

I love my mom.

And Debbie.

And these fluffy little turtles.

Skill #101:

The Easiest Bread in the World

In November 2006, *New York Times* food columnist Mark Bittman wrote an article for his Sunday feature—it was just an interview with a baker who came up with a new method to bake bread, no big deal. Except that this baker claimed he had not only developed a manner of making absolutely amazing bread at home without the headaches of kneading and working the dough, but that his process was so easy, a four-year-old could do it.

Wait. Why would a commercial baker develop a way to make his product at home? This seemed a little self-defeating. But this baker—his name was Jim Lahey—stated that his goal was for anyone to be able to create bakery-quality bread—you know, that bread with the hard crust and the rich center, not the squishy store-bought stuff—as often as they wanted.

So, Mark Bittman met with Lahey and the two baked this new bread together. Bittman wrote the piece and that article launched an entire bread-making movement. There were videos, additional articles, online pieces, cookbooks—all about this new method of baking bread easily.

Now, baking bread had always been a daunting and intimidating task, one only taken on by the serious home baker. It was time-consuming, required a lot of attention, and was easy to mess up—which is why homemade bread has always been so revered.

The traditional process of baking bread requires dissolving yeast and sugar in water, then adding in lard, salt, and flour. Then the kneading starts. After that, the bread has to rise for an hour. Then you punch the dough and allow it to deflate and sit for another hour. Then you bake.

Then, in the 1990s, bread machines came along. These things were great. Now there was a machine where you could load in all the ingredients and allow the device to do all the kneading, punching, waiting, and cooking. You just loaded it up, pressed a few buttons, and walked away. But the bread was still the soft, squishy store-bought kind—a much fresher, preservative-free version of it, but still not that artisan, bakery-style bread we all love.

Then came Jim Lahey's method, where we can not only make the most amazing artisan bread ever, but it is so incredibly easy that—yes, a four-year-old can do it.

What Jim Lahey came up with was a way to allow *time* to do all the work—up to twenty-four hours. It takes a minute to mix the bread, uses only a quarter teaspoon of yeast (most recipes call for a full teaspoon or more), and allows the yeast to ferment very slowly. The dough is so sticky that you couldn't knead it even if you wanted to, which is good because you just leave it alone and let it do its thing.

His method creates a great cracking crust and flavor and is the kind of bread that you get from professionals' steam-injected ovens. And it does this by allowing the pot you cook it in to act as a steam oven and get the same results. Over the past year, I've made dozens of loaves of this bread, and with a few tweaks, it's pretty bulletproof.

So how do you make no-knead bread? It's pretty easy. First, you will need:

1 ¾ cup of warm water
3 cups of flour
1 teaspoon of salt
¼ teaspoon of yeast

1. In a large bowl combine the flour, yeast, and salt. Mix the dry ingredients, then add your water. Cover the bowl with plastic wrap and let it sit. Jim Lahey's recipe calls for between eighteen and twenty-four hours, but I would say eight hours is a minimum. I make a batch up at night and we have it for breakfast the next day. I also use a Sharpie and write on the plastic wrap the time that I started it, so I don't forget. If you like a larger loaf and less dense bread, wait longer, toward the twenty-four-hour time frame.

2. Place flour over a cutting board and place the dough on it. Fold it into a ball—don't knead it or work it; just fold it—place back in the bowl and cover back with plastic wrap for thirty minutes.

3. Hint: What I do here is, while the dough is on the cutting board, I wash out the bowl, dry it, and place a layer of olive oil on the bottom. Then when the dough goes back in the bowl, I'll add a little olive oil on the top. This will add flavor and allow the bread to easily slip into the pan when you cook it.

4. Preheat the oven to 400 degrees and place a Dutch oven, casserole dish, or anything that has a heavy cover and seals, into the oven to preheat—empty—for ten minutes. You want the pan to be hot when you start.

5. Place the bread inside the Dutch oven. I used to cut vent holes on the top of the loaf, but I found that they don't

do much and the look of the bread is nicer without them. Cook for thirty minutes.

6. Remove the lid and cook for an additional five minutes or so to get the top get crusty.

It's tempting to cut the bread right out of the oven, but you get a better result if you let it cool for ten minutes or so.

Now, I might add that with this recipe everything depends on the Dutch oven or pot that you use to cook it in. With mine, I can't get the crust extremely crusty without burning the bottom of the bread, so I settle for a medium crust. I've seen others do it where they can cook an extra five minutes or so and get the bread crusty all over. You can try adding parchment paper to the bottom of the pot; that will give you some additional cooking time.

And that's it. No-knead bread. Fast, easy, fun, and cheap to make. Obviously, there are no preservatives in it like there are with store-bought bread, so it won't stay fresh for more than a week or so, but you won't have to worry about it. This bread goes fast. We've never had a loaf make it to three days.

Two days is our record—two days, five hours, and sixteen minutes.

Velma

My mother, Velma, invented the Egg McMuffin.

This would have been around 1957, at a business she owned with her father called the Gem Diner.

The Gem Diner was a little place in Sanitaria Springs, New York—which in itself was a little place near Binghamton, New York—that sat on the side of Route 7 and sold sandwiches, shakes, burgers, and fries to travelers who would stop by for lunch or an early dinner. But few people came in for breakfast.

"They stop and get coffee," Velma said to her father.

"They get coffee," Grover corrected, "to go. They don't want to be late for work, so they fill their thermos and leave."

So, Velma began thinking of a portable breakfast that could be made quickly. She came up with a fried egg, slice of Canadian bacon, and cheese served on a toasted English muffin.

"What is it?" Grover felt the warmth of the English muffin and egg flow through the wax paper that covered the sandwich.

"It's breakfast."

"Well," he said as he unwrapped it. "We'll give it a try."

They sold out the first week. The item was named the Gem Diner Special and it cost thirty cents.

"Don't forget the Gem Diner Special tomorrow," Grover would remind every customer he rang out.

Now, on the road from Bainbridge, New York, to Binghamton, New York, there were more than fifteen places to stop and get a cup of coffee on your way home from work— twenty, if you weren't picky. But none of them had a prettier waitress than Velma. So, every day Larry De Morier stopped at the Gem Diner. Every day he would talk to Velma. And every day he would leave—only after he had made her laugh at least twice.

He proposed to her on the porch steps of Grover's house in Sanitaria Springs—just around the corner from the diner. They were married in January 1958. Grover rented the upstairs rooms out to people, so he moved to a back bedroom of the house, and the newlyweds took the first floor.

Four years later, two days after Christmas in 1962, Velma awoke suddenly and knew it was time to deliver her child. She woke her husband, who carried her bag out and scrambled to get her into the car. Larry jumped in—it was ten miles to the hospital, but the roads would be clear at this hour—but when he turned the car key, nothing happened. He tried again. And again. Without even a click from the starter to signify effort, the car did not start.

Larry jumped out of the car—leaving his wife inside— and disappeared. It was cold and silent in Sanitaria Springs at that time of night. Velma sat, trying to remain calm, until she heard the roar of a large engine in the distance and saw a car racing toward her: a copper-colored Ford Fairlane. Larry jumped out to transfer his wife inside.

"Whose car is this?" she asked, through shallow breaths.

"A friend's."

Larry shot out of the stone driveway.

On the clear back roads, they made good time. They got to the hospital, their child was born, and fifteen hours later—when his head had finally cleared—Larry decided he'd better find out whose car it was he had taken. He had run up the street and looked inside every car he passed until he came across one with the keys in it.

He and Grover made some phone calls, identified the owner of the car, described the situation to a very understanding neighbor. The police were contacted and they called off their search for the stolen Fairlane.

The Gem Diner did well for a few more years, but the hours were long and demanding. And Grover decided it was too much for his daughter and her young family—and too much for him. They closed the doors.

Grover paced the big house trying to determine what do next—especially since Larry and Velma would soon have another mouth to feed, with their second child on the way. Grover had to come up with a source of income for her where she wouldn't have to be away from home so much. He had an idea.

"A fish store?" Velma asked. "You mean, fish to eat?"

"No. Tropical fish," he said excitedly, pointing to the area that had once been the bar of the old hotel. "Right here. You wouldn't even have to leave the house to take care of customers. You would hear the buzzer inside the house when someone came in that door, and you would just walk in through the house. Simple."

Grover got to work on the Mermaid Aquarium, Sanitaria Springs' first tropical fish store. He bought display cases and shelving, hoses, and tank decorations, and filled more than a hundred different tanks with water, gravel, pumps, and exotic fish.

"Do people care about tropical fish?" Velma asked.

"You'll make them care. And a fish tank is cheaper than one of them color TVs, remind them of that."

Grover walked out to his car, motioning for his son-in-law to help him carry something back in.

"What is it?" Larry lifted his side of the box but something inside moved.

"Alligators."

"What?"

"Baby ones. Put them in that tank right next to the piranhas."

Preparations for the store continued. And two days before the grand opening of the Mermaid Aquarium, Grover died. Velma opened the store without him. And a week after that, she named her new daughter after her father's favorite song: Laura.

The Mermaid Aquarium provided a solid second income to the family, and with the rent from the tenants upstairs and Larry's small salary, they squeaked by. In fact, there were even a few dollars to spend on a new trend: kids' birthday parties hosted at McDonald's.

In 1972, as Velma watched kids at the Front Street McDonald's—where they had games, music, and cake set up for her son's tenth birthday—she passed a large poster with an announcement: The franchise would now start serving breakfast and invited everyone to try the brand-new Egg McMuffin.

Velma smiled.

I thought of these stories as I helped her pack to move. I thought of how, when my dad went on medical disability in 1978 and his small salary grew even smaller, Velma became the oldest college freshman at the State University of New York at Delhi's nursing program. She was fifty-four years old and she combined classes and graduated in one year. She then went to work at the Delaware Valley Hospital in Walton for almost thirty years, where she won Nurse of the Year in 2002. A plaque still hangs there with her name on it.

We continued to pack.

"Not everything," she told me. "We don't need to take everything, just a few things. I'll be back."

"I know."

And we would be back—a few times, to get the house ready to sell.

"Your heart is strong, Velma," Dr. Freeman had said, only a few days earlier, when he examined her. "Very strong. So are your legs. But your balance is terrible."

So, Velma would go to Ohio, to Laura's house, where there was a room waiting for her, until we could find an assisted living facility where she could have her things and join the kind of groups and organizations that she loved.

"I'm not just going to twiddle my thumbs," Velma said.

"No one is asking you to."

"I need to do things."

"We know."

And we packed her bag and got her medication. We took a few of her pictures and I checked the lock twice. We got in the car and then went back inside for her cane—she didn't think she would need it. Then we adjusted the heat in the car to volcanic levels—just the way she likes it—and we headed out for the five-hour drive to meet my sister halfway between Walton and Columbus.

"I didn't get breakfast," Velma announced, as if a serious crime had been committed against her.

"We'll stop at McDonald's on the way out."

"Okay."

And we did. We got two Egg McMuffins.

Skill #353:

How to Change the Oil in Your Car

The year 1971 was a very unique one. Charles Manson was convicted for his part in the Tate-LaBianca murders. Paul McCartney formed a new band called Wings. A man calling himself D. B. Cooper hijacked a Boeing 727 and then parachuted from the plane with two hundred thousand dollars in ransom cash. And at Madison Square Garden, Joe Frazier defeated the great Muhammad Ali.

It was also the year of Edwin Washburn.

Edwin Washburn was man who, when he retired from the military, finally had the long-awaited back surgery he had been putting off. And as Edwin was recuperating, he wondered how he would get down under his vehicles to change the oil now that his mobility was limited.

In a tire store, Washburn noticed that there was an outside pit where mechanics could work on campers and RVs. Why couldn't you do this inside, with cars, and by doing it, drastically reduce the service time? And from this idea, the very first Jiffy Lube fast-oil-change shop was born.

Now, these shops would have remained simply a few unique stores in Utah if it wasn't for another character named Jim Hindman.

Hindman was a successful businessman and was also the football coach at Western Maryland College. During a conversation on tenacity and a good work ethic, one of his players spoke up.

"That's great, coach, but you already made your million. I'd like to see you make another one."

So, he did. Hindman purchased the first Jiffy Lube from Washburn and began spinning out franchises.

According to the last published count in 2015, there are 1,918 Jiffy Lube locations, and an additional eight hundred Valvoline Instant Oil change centers, making the instant oil-change shop a solid part of the car maintenance landscape.

Now, this is both a good and a bad thing. It's good because the instant oil-change sites have probably extended the life of many cars for drivers who would never change their own oil and who don't have the funds or time for an oil change at the dealer or their local mechanic. But the downside is that now the concept of changing your own oil is right up there with grinding your own meat or making your own clothes because today there are generations of drivers who have never owned a car during a time when you couldn't pull in during lunch for a fifteen-minute oil change.

But changing the oil in your own car is not only something that's easy to do, but it puts a little control back in your auto-owning life. It's a simple maintenance task that you can master easily.

So, how do you change the oil in your car?

Well, the first rule: Get yourself a good set of car ramps—those metal ramps you see in the auto department of Walmart. Never, ever use the car jack.

I mean it. Don't use the car jack.

You can get a decent set of ramps for forty bucks that will last you a lifetime, so don't use the car jack for anything other than roadside emergencies.

That jack that came with your car was meant to lift the vehicle just high enough to change your tire during an emergency. It was never designed to lift the car up for maintenance. The higher the car goes, the more unstable it is, and the easier it becomes to get hurt—especially if you're yanking at a stubborn oil filter on an already-unstable three-thousand-pound vehicle. Also, if you place the car jack in the wrong place, you can do some serious damage to your car.

With that out of the way, let's cover the basic steps:

Go to an auto parts or department store and get the oil and oil filter for your car—there should be guides there to tell you what you need, or you can find that information in the car's owner's manual. You will also need a pan to catch the old oil, a socket set, and an oil filter wrench—all inexpensive and easily found.

Open the car's hood and remove the oil cap, which should be clearly marked, usually around the center of the engine. This will allow the oil from the crankcase—which is the cavity where the oil shaft of the car lives—to drain easier.

Drive the car up onto the ramps—after you've put the hood back down, of course, so you can see where you're going—and apply the emergency brake.

Drain the oil. Once you get under the car you will see a flat metal pan with a square plug—the perfect size for the end of a socket wrench to fit in. Place the drip pan on the ground, directly under that plug. Unscrew the plug and remove it. Oil will drain out and into the pan. When the oil has drained completely—and this could take a few minutes—replace the plug.

Remove the oil filter. The filter is easy to find on the side of the engine block, which is the lower, larger part of the engine. Unscrew it and remove it, making sure you take off the rubber gasket of the filter as well.

Replace the filter. Dip the tip of your finger in the new oil and run it along the gasket of the new filter. This will help create a tighter seal. Screw on the new filter.

Add in the new oil back into the crankcase. Replace the oil cap. Start the engine and make sure the oil pressure light turns on and your oil pressure gauge moves.

And that's it.

And yes, I know, the oil-change place around the corner charges around twenty bucks to change your oil and you can stay right in your car while they do it, checking all those important emails you received and looking at dog pictures on Facebook. But it's not the same. Knowing how to change your oil gives you the option to do so. It gives you the choice: Do I do it myself, or pay someone else to do it? You get to choose.

Two Good Men

One Saturday afternoon, I learned that a man I had known for many years had died. Shortly after that, I found out that another man I had known for many years had died as well.

These two men did not know each other. They lived in different towns in different states and they probably never would have met. But they both died within an hour of each other—one after battling cancer and the other completely without warning.

These were both good men. Great men. Men who left this world the same way that they lived in it—John, while helping out a friend, and Kirk, while being surrounded by his family.

And these two people who had never met—these solid Christians who were rooted in their beliefs and demonstrated their faith in all ways—arrived in heaven on the same day.

Now I don't know what your beliefs are, but mine are that these two men are in heaven. I know this is true and I know that heaven is real. And this is what John and Kirk both knew to be true.

John Risner was probably one of the most giving men I had ever known. He was the guy behind the scenes, the ghost that you always just caught sight of as he was carrying away a paintbrush or loading up a lawnmower just minutes after you got there. He was one who never sought attention and whose humble sweat just got stuff done.

John and his wife, Tina, donated hundreds of hours to the church. They were both heavily involved with the children's youth program and John was the church properties director. And they both had taken vacation time to go on a mission trip to the Dominican Republic.

John died while giving up his Saturday to help a young couple from the church. They had just bought a house and were fixing it up, and John was on a ladder pulling the last piece of aluminum siding off. He lost his footing and fell.

John did everything right—he had people holding the ladder from below, he had the right angle, and he wasn't reaching too far. No one could have predicted the accident. Which meant that John didn't have time from the top of the ladder to the bottom to think about his life. When John died, it just happened. He didn't get to lie on his deathbed for days contemplating his life, his mortality, and if there was an afterlife. He didn't then decide to make a spiritual commitment or not.

Kirk Darville had that time, but he didn't need it. He had made that decision decades earlier. It showed all around him. He demonstrated it while he was the pastor of his small church and during his career as a schoolteacher. He was lighthearted and happy and was always there to patch something up or fix something at my elderly mother's house—accepting pennies on the dollar from what the work really should have cost.

Kirk's faith was solid, and although he didn't want to leave this world and fought to stay with the people he loved, he knew there was a better place waiting for him.

I know these two men are in heaven. And I know that I will see these two men again. Because I know where they are, and I know where I am going.

But still, when I heard they had died, I was sad.

Sad for the people they have left and sad for the hole that remains now that John and Kirk are gone.

There is a big empty place left without them.

It remains empty because something so big was once there.

How to Make Acorn Pancakes

When I was a kid, my all-time favorite book—and I mean all-time favorite—was a novel entitled *My Side of the Mountain*. I loved that book and read it at least a dozen times. It's the story of a boy named Sam—I think he was around twelve years old—who runs away from his New York City home and heads for the Catskill Mountains to live off the land. The book actually takes place in Delhi, New York, which is sixteen miles from my hometown of Walton.

Now, Sam isn't the typical runaway. He doesn't hate his parents. He's not in trouble with the law. And he is not being abused. He just wants to be on his own and wants to live in the mountains.

So he does.

While surviving alone, he hollows out the base of a tree to live in, raises a baby peregrine falcon that he trains to hunt for him, and has some other amazing adventures.

For food, Sam survives on the rabbits and squirrels that Frightful—Sam's trained falcon—brings him, as well as the occasional stolen deer poached from the illegal hunters who shot them out of season. And of course, there were acorn pancakes. Sam lived on piles and piles of acorn pancakes.

Now, when I was a kid, I asked my mother if we could make acorn pancakes, and she told me it was impossible. She said *My Side of the Mountain* was simply a story; you couldn't make flour from acorns, and therefore, you couldn't make pancakes from acorn flour.

I was heartbroken. The author had lied to me! Everything else had seemed so real. . . . Years later, when I had finally come to grips with forgiving author Jean Craighead George for her deception, I discovered that she was not the one lying. (Sorry, Mom!) There are acorn pancakes.

Acorn pancakes and acorn biscuits were actually a staple of the Native American diet. Acorns hold some valuable proteins and carbohydrates and also had a good deal of saturated fat. In the modern world, acorns are fun to collect, fun to process, and they add a unique nutty flavor to food that can't be found anywhere else.

So how do you make acorn pancakes? It's somewhat labor intensive, but it's fun to do.

The first step is to collect your acorns, and the rule of thumb here is to harvest a third more than you need. The acorns should be perfect specimens—if they are rotten or have been infiltrated by bugs, don't use them.

You need to crack the acorns and get to the meat. This is where you'll do your final inspection. If the nuts are dark, chipped, or look as if bugs have gotten in, chuck them.

Once you have everything sorted, you need to chop up the nuts. A coffee grinder works well for this. You don't want to get the acorn meal down to a flour consistency, but more like the consistency of ground coffee beans.

If you were to taste the acorn meal right now, you would notice one thing: It's horrible.

That's because it's loaded with tannins. Native Americans would take the acorns and fill baskets with them and leave them in streams. It's difficult to get the tannins out, but crucial. The method I've found that works the best is to use a stocking. Take a piece of cheesecloth or a nylon stocking and fill it with the acorn meal. Tie it off and run it under cold water, all the time kneading the stocking. You'll need to do this several times—a dozen or so—to make sure the tannins are all out. A good way to check is to taste the water that comes out of the meal you are rinsing. If it's clear and has no taste, you're good.

Some people bake the acorn meal, but I find this gives it a bitter taste. Just spread it out and let it dry.

Now, there is no yeast in acorn meal, so it's best to add it to other kinds of flour. I like using buckwheat flour or cornmeal. This will give the flour a unique nutty and sweet flavor.

So, now you have the acorn meal and from this comes the pancakes.

You will need:

½ cup white flour
1 cup of acorn meal
2½ teaspoons baking powder
¾ teaspoon salt
1 egg, beaten
1¼ cups milk
3 tablespoons oil

Mix all the ingredients together—it's up to you whether you mix by hand or with a mixer, since that kind of lumpiness adds to it. Spoon whatever amount of batter you need to make a pancake in your preferred size onto a hot greased pan. Wait two to three minutes, then flip once. When it cooks on the other side, you're done.

Knowing how to make acorn pancakes is not a mission-critical skill to possess. It's not up there with being able to change your tire or tie a necktie. But it's a fun thing to do with your kids as a fall project or just as a creative way to zest up foods, while also taking advantage of all those free acorns lying around in your yard.

Now, if you are unlucky enough to live somewhere where you don't have a yard full of oak trees, you are more than welcome to come to my place in the fall and take as many acorns as you want. I am also running a sale on leaves.

The Need for
One Good Thermos

There are a handful of items that everyone needs to own—not *should* own but *needs* to own. These objects are not a suggestion, not simply a list that would be nice once we get around to it. They are the gear that is part of the required inventory of life—the unwritten rules that define the daily system.

And because these objects need to be part of our possessions, they should be a part of sons' and grandsons' inventory as they grow up. Our children may not remember what video game they received, but they both will remember who gave them their first pocket knife, their first wallet, and their first watch.

Now, this list—the required list of things for the man inventory—includes the following items:

:: One good pocket knife—a decent one, in the forty-dollar range

:: One silver money clip—yes, you can still keep your wallet, but there is something not only stylish about a money clip, but there's a definite advantage of physically seeing the cash you have left

:: One set of inexpensive but reliable hand tools

:: One reliable wristwatch

:: And one high-quality thermos

In this brand-conscious world, you may think that the word *thermos* is a misnomer because it describes the company, not the product—just like Kleenex or Xerox—because the actual item is called a "vacuum bottle" or "vacuum flask." But in 1963, the United States declared *thermos* to be a "genericized trademark" and the term is actually now synonymous with vacuum bottles.

So, feel free to use the word *thermos* as much as you want.

The first glass-lined bottle was invented in 1892 by a German physicist named James Dewar, who came up with the idea of a bottle within a bottle that was at first referred to as the Dewar flask or Dewar bottle. Between the outside layer of the thermos and the inside is a vacuum of air that prohibits the liquid from getting out. The heat—or cold—becomes trapped inside.

Now, because of the popularity of the thermos, you would think that James Dewar became a very wealthy man. But Dewar never registered a patent for his invention and it was subsequently patented and produced by—yup, the Thermos company, which rolled it out in 1907 for commercial use by the truckload.

The thermos changed everything. In a time when commercial refrigeration was still decades away and microwaves were pure science fiction, a thermos could transport hot or cold liquids for hours. In fact, when World War II broke out in Europe, the Thermos company turned all its English production to the war effort. Every time a British bombing run went out, the men were equipped with a thermos full of hot coffee or soup.

Now, in our modern world, a good thermos is handier than you might realize. By taking a thermos full of coffee to work every day instead of stopping at Starbucks, you can save over a thousand dollars a year. Also, the waste is drastically reduced—how many half-cups of cold coffee do you throw out every year? With a thermos, only the coffee you've poured into the cap or a cup is exposed, and the remaining liquid stays warm in the bottle. Many times, I'm still drinking my morning coffee out of my thermos in the afternoon. And a thermos can be used for more than just coffee or tea. A wide-mouth thermos is great for carrying soups and stews. And how can you compare a lunch of bologna and cheese to one of a piping-hot cup of homemade soup with crackers? Yeah, it's a little more muss and fuss, but it's a heartier meal.

For the outdoorsman, sitting in a tree stand or standing in a cold trout stream, a thermos of hot coffee is mandatory. And for those of us who spend most of their time in a car, a thermos is not only financially attractive, but drastically cuts down on the number of coffee stops we need to make—though the number of bathroom breaks remains the same.

Of course, there is a world of difference between a thermos and a good thermos.

A simple thermos can be purchased from a dollar store and is actually just a glorified travel mug: a thick plastic bottle with a cap. It will keep your liquids warm for an hour at best. And stainless-steel bottles are pretty much the same thing—a metal container that lacks that vacuum layer to keep the liquid hot or cold.

So, how do you tell if a thermos is high in quality and where can you buy one?

There are many high-quality thermos brands but for years the top two were always Thermos and Stanley. You can find these brands almost anywhere, but my advice is that the best way to find them is to buy used. The older brands with the glass liners work great and are relatively indestructible—though, depending on the brand, they can still break. You can find these at every yard sale and thrift store for only a few bucks.

Once you have your thermos, there's only one rule when it comes to using it: Prime it first. That is, before you pour in the hot coffee or soup, fill the thermos with hot water first and let the inside bottle warm up. It only takes a few minutes to do this. With a good thermos, the heat of your priming water will drastically increase the length of time the liquid will stay warm. I know several guys who microwave a few cups of water until it boils and use that to prime the thermos. These are the guys who can actually get their coffee to stay warm for twenty-four hours—my personal record is about eight.

A good thermos will run you about thirty bucks, can be found at any Target or Walmart, and should last a long time.

Skill #333:

How to Create a Budget

When my wife, Debbie, and I were first married, we were on a very strict budget—I mean a death grip budget—where every dime was needed and every penny was accounted for. And even though we were extremely strict with our money, we didn't go without. We didn't go hungry and we didn't go into debt. In fact, it was not even a difficult financial time for us, just more of a disciplined one—a lean but happy time. Actually, it was because our household budget was so severe that this was an extremely secure and safe time for us—because no matter what happened financially, we had a budget envelope set aside for it.

Now, my routine at that time was pretty set as well. Every payday, I would leave work at lunch to cash my check, and when I did, I had the guilty pleasure of peeling off the very top seven dollars—we had calculated both our checks down to what was needed and mine held an extra seven bucks in it—and I would get to just blow that money. The bulk of the check was converted into cash to be taken home and placed in the various envelopes where it was needed, but that first seven bucks, that top seven bucks, was all mine, baby. And that meant I could spend it on . . . any . . . thing . . . I . . . wanted.

And I did.

It took me about nine minutes.

Because the bank we used on Court Street in Binghamton, New York, was only a block away from the greatest delicatessen north of Flatbush: the Old World Deli. And every Friday, I would wait in line with the downtown lunch crowd along with the smells of pastrami and corned beef and I would order a sandwich the size of my head, a pickle, and a drink. And even though I would try to make the lunch last, even though I would try to savor it, the meal would be over in less than ten minutes. And once again I would be broke.

Happy, but broke.

Now, this type of severe budgeting is not a great way to plan because it breaks the first financial rule of pay yourself first—and pay yourself more than seven dollars. It also shows what happens when you are ultra-strict about your finances—and what happens when you do get a few bucks in your pocket.

But it worked for us.

The main rule in creating a budget is this: Cash is king.

The best and most pure method of creating a budget is to use a cash system. A simple cash envelope system—keeping separate envelopes marked with each budget area and then placing the cash needed in each envelope—is the best method by far. No math errors. No confusion. If you don't have enough money in the envelope, then you don't have enough money for that item.

As a side note, most homeowner's insurance policies won't cover cash above around five hundred dollars, so, if you're going to keep more than that around the house, you may want to get a fireproof safe to protect it.

Whether we like it or not, we are very close to becoming a cashless society. Our paychecks are directly deposited. Many of us pay bills electronically, and we use our debit or credit cards to buy most of the items we need. Electronic bits and bytes bounce back and forth the way dollars and coins once did. In fact, many economists estimate that paper checks may be completely obsolete by 2020.

On top of that, we are becoming a society that is not only e-payment friendly but actually cash-resistant. The business world doesn't want you to use cash.

Why?

Well, from the merchant's perspective, the less cash a business takes in means less risk of error or theft. It also means there is less need to make physical bank deposits, and if you are purchasing from a line of credit, your buying power has increased. So, a merchant sells less to those using cash than those using a line of credit.

From a banking perspective, credit-card interest is a financial goldmine, but even using debit cards makes banks a lot of money—I mean, a lot of money. Every time you use your debit card as a credit card, the merchant pays a bank fee. And every time you use the debit card as a debit card, the bank will either charge you a POS (point of sale) fee or build in a monthly cost into your account. In fact, many banks are raising these POS fees to discourage consumers from using the cards as debit cards, because they can make so much more income by charging the merchants for the credit transaction.

And there's also the government's point of view for preferring credit over cash. Having all payments electronically ensures that all transactions are recorded—and can be taxed.

From a consumer perspective, it's simply becoming easier to use credit or debit cards than to have to carry around lots of cash. We can now use cards in vending machines and in parking meters, and many stores have drastically dropped—or completely eliminated—minimum purchase amounts on credit and debit cards, which means we can buy a pack of gum or a soda and put it on a card. And because our paycheck is often direct-deposited, using our debit card saves us the chore of running to the bank or ATM.

So, how do we create a cash budget in a cashless society?

Well, the best way is to use cash in those areas where we have the most flexibility—and, therefore, the largest margin for error.

First, get organized. Grab all your bills, statements, and other account data and begin listing all your expenses—not only monthly expenses. If you pay something once or twice a year, you need to remember to set aside a portion for that each month. Include in this list everything: car insurance, mortgage or rent, car payments, entertainment, groceries, utilities, dry cleaning, garbage services, car maintenance, retirement or college savings, vacations. Everything.

Next, gather data about the money you have coming in. List all your monthly income. Record all of your sources of income—if you do something once or twice a year that earns income, include that along with your regular income.

Then, break down the expenses. Everything you owe is in one of two categories: It's either fixed—meaning it is the same payment month after month—or it is variable— meaning the amount of the expense can change, such as groceries, entertainment, vacations, and so on. Use cash for all your variable expenses.

Total everything up. If your total for expenses is less than the total for income, good. We're off to a great start. This means you will have some wiggle room to whittle down any debt you have or save and invest. If your list shows more expenses going out than income coming in, you'll need to make some changes. Usually, this kind of situation is tied to a high debt load, so look at that first and see what can be done to reduce it.

Adjust, adjust, adjust. It will take about three months to tweak your budget so it works for you. There will be items you forgot or things you need to change. The more accurate the budget is, the more of a tool it will be for you.

And remember: You don't need a high income to have financial security. The more you budget and stay out of debt, the better off you will be. My cousin, Rena, was the sole breadwinner of her family. She bought a house, raised two kids, put them both through college, and has a nice retirement lined up—all on the salary of a McDonald's manager.

The Bar

On Sunday, February 4, 2007—the day of Super Bowl XLI—our house in Vestal, New York, was empty.

The wooden floors that had been protected by rugs and furniture for over a decade were shiny and bare. The walls—including the ones that Debbie had made me paint twice when she changed her mind on the color—were decorated only with outlines where picture frames had blocked the sun. Rooms whose every noise and bump we had once known now bounced strange sounds through their empty spaces.

The new job I had accepted came with a complete relocation package, which included a team of packers and movers who marched in and took our entire life—beds, bicycles, furniture, the kids' toys, clothes, and eleven years' worth of living—and squeezed it all into one single truck: two hundred eight square feet of moving space. Or fifty-two square feet per person in our household. Or a little over nineteen square feet for every year we had lived there. And all that life, all that stuff, was now parked in a storage lot for a week, until we could close on our new house, two states away.

So, we would leave the town where Debbie and I had first met—at the health club a few blocks from our house—and where our wedding reception had been held—at the Vestal Steakhouse on the Vestal Parkway—and we would leave the area we had known for years, leave the neighborhood, the family, and the familiar.

But first, we would go to the Super Bowl/going-away party at Jennifer and Dave's house next door. The entire neighborhood would be there and we would say our good-byes and then we would come home to our own house one last time. We would climb into our sleeping bags, spread out on top of air mattresses, and we would sleep. And then in the morning, we would leave.

And that house at 317 Frey Avenue in Vestal—the place that had been home for eleven years—would belong to someone else.

Now, when we first bought the house—this was back in 1996—the move was so much simpler than this one. Going from our small apartment to the house was incredibly easy. It only took my cousin Brad and me a few hours. Plus, we were only a family of three then—Nick was a toddler and Alex hadn't been born yet and we actually wondered how we would ever fill up that big house.

That first night that we spent in our new Vestal home, back in 1996, Debbie and I had sat in the living room together. We had put Nick to bed and were watching *Aladdin*—the cable wouldn't get turned on until the following week and we only owned kids' videotapes. It was then that Debbie made the announcement.

"Go get us wings."

Now, in Endicott, where our old apartment had been located—clear across the Susquehanna River—there were plenty of places to get chicken wings, and Debbie and I had become complete wing snobs over the years. But we were in Vestal now.

"Where?"

"I don't know. Go find a place."

Finding a place for good chicken wings in Upstate New York is not as difficult as you might think. It's like trying to find a good show in Vegas or a great fishing spot in Maine. The corner bar and grill would always have the best food and there were hundreds of them around. So, I got in the car and drove.

And that's when I found the Terrace.

The place was packed inside when I walked in, but I made my way up to the bar.

"You look lost," Lynn the bartender said over the noise of the jukebox and the crowd. She was smiling.

"Yeah, I might be. How are your wings?"

She gave me a look that was a combination of "What, are you stupid?" mixed with "Don't insult me by asking." I ordered two dozen wings to go and sat at the bar and nursed a beer while I waited.

I would return again and again for the next eleven years.

At least once a week we got wings or sandwiches or some other food from the Terrace—and of course, you had to go there to order it. Actually, you could call it in, but that would remove the time at the bar, waiting, talking, and soaking it all in. And I became a regular. The Terrace became my bar and I became a part of it. I never stayed late; I was always home by six o'clock—plenty of time for dinner with Debbie and the kids. Or I would bring dinner home with me from there. And I was rarely at the bar on weekends—just once or twice a week for a few hours, the minimum amount of time required to hold my place in the pack. Just enough to keep the bar a part of me and me a part of it.

Now, everyone has a role to play at a bar. You have your expert on everything—Mike. You have your big shots—Chris the lawyer and Jimmy the broker. You have the pack leaders—Big Frank and Remmy. You had borderline criminals—Newt and the Haircut Guy (he only came in on the days he got his hair cut). And you had a potpourri of assorted bar characters.

At the Terrace, I got to play the part of the writer. This was a fun role that required very little work and absolutely no writing.

I cried at the Terrace. But I laughed there, too. And I always left before I really wanted to, and I did this from 1996 to 2007. During that time, I belonged to the Terrace and it belonged to me.

And then 2007 came and we moved away.

And although I thought about the bar—a lot—I never went back, not even when I'd be passing through the area. I guess I was afraid of seeing something spoiled or ruined. So I avoided it.

Until last month.

I was in town heading to Syracuse for a meeting and didn't want to drive any farther, so I checked into the Hampton Inn on the Vestal Parkway and headed over to the Terrace for wings.

It's humbling to go back to places that were once important to you. Just because you left, you expect them to wind down and stop, but they continue. And there are all new faces, with all new groups, and they come with a different pecking order and a new gauge of respect and esteem. You want to grab these people and tell them that you were part of this once, too—that you sat where they sat and you passed the same tests they did, and that there was a time when your group—not theirs—was important to this place.

It's sad when time moves on without you.

But it's even sadder when it doesn't.

I had just walked through the door of the Terrace and was working my way toward one of the many empty barstools when I heard my name called. Then I heard it again. And again.

After all these years, they were all still there: Mike, Sam, Big Frank, Remmy, Lynn. All of them.

They were all still there.

I sat at the bar and ordered my wings. The backslaps and the handshakes started. And then those little blue plastic chips began to build up around my beer glass—indicating that someone had just bought you a drink: *This one is from Mike. This is from big Frank.*

I took my position back.

I learned that the great crowds are now gone from the Terrace. The once-strong blue-collar area where it is located has greatly dwindled in numbers, with most of the coveted, high-paying factory and manufacturing jobs all but vanished. Many of the buildings nearby are empty, some with broken windows and grass growing through employee parking lots that once held hundreds of employees' cars and trucks. So, even though the bar's large crowds had moved on, the people at the Terrace who once held court over them have remained at their post.

Since I moved, I had found the time to finally finish that book I was always talking about. It won a few awards and was actually being taught in schools. And although they all knew about it, they teased and congratulated me, but those accolades didn't give me back the emotional dividend I had always expected they would.

It wasn't that I had *moved on* from the Terrace. I hadn't. I had just . . . *moved.* I had cheated. I didn't graduate or wake up one day and no longer need the place. I just took the bar out of the equation. If we hadn't moved, if I hadn't evaded that decision, would I still be there, too?

I never found a similar local bar in Dover, where we live now. I remember looking for one when we first arrived, but to tell the truth, I didn't look very hard.

I don't regret my time at the Terrace, but I don't yearn for it, either. That might be maturity. But I doubt it.

It's just that, over time, you begin to see the beauty in the unassuming parts of life: work, writing, the house. Older men crave all of these things—we thrive on it. We hunt it. Older men need results.

Younger men don't.

Younger men need bars, where all you need to do is dream about something. Brag about it. And promise to one day claim it.

And if you do that, then it's real.

Skill #11:

Using the Yankee Drill

A Yankee drill—also known as a Yankee screwdriver or a push drill—is not only a must-have for every person who owns a tool box, but is also one of the best-kept secrets when it comes to hand tools.

I say this with some amount of verifiable data because, when we had our house fire a few years ago, the Yankee drill was the one item that kept flummoxing Liberty Insurance's computers when the company was trying to establish a replacement value.

"A what kind of drill?"

The Yankee drill has been around since the mid-1800s and is one of the earliest forms of handheld drills. It is a mechanical tool; it looks like a long stick with a handle on one end that has a rotating end that is flat but when you set it against a flat surface and press against it, the drill rotates in the shaft and into the surface.

Now, you won't see commercials about Yankee drills. There will not be huge displays at Lowe's, it won't be a NASCAR sponsor, and your neighbor won't ask you to come over and check out the new Yankee drill he just got.

Why? Because there's nothing really sexy about them and they've been around forever.

Which is one of the best reasons to own one. They are simple, time-tested, reliable, will last you a lifetime (unless you burn your house down), and will also save you an enormous amount of time.

But, you may ask, if I have a cordless drill, why would I need a hundred-and-fifty-year-old handheld drill?

Great question. And here is one answer: pilot holes.

Picture this. You are putting up a set of vertical blinds— I'm using this as an example because I hate putting up vertical blinds.

Here's the normal process:

With the vertical blinds, there will be small plastic boxes that hold the blind to the window frame. Place the blind where you want it on the window frame, which will show you where the ends are. Place each box on the end, so you can mark where they go.

Mark the holes with a pencil.

Take your cordless drill and insert a drill bit.

Drill the pilot holes (a fancy name for that smaller hole drilled into the wood so your screw can follow it) on the pencil marks.

Replace the drill bit with the screwdriver bit.

Use the cordless screwdriver to screw in the hardware.

With a Yankee drill, the process gets much simpler: You repeat the first step—align the blind and place the boxes where you need them. But then, instead of marking them with a pencil, just take your Yankee drill and drill in pilot holes. Then screw the boxes to the window frame.

Done.

Think of every time you need to drill a pilot hole. You can now use a Yankee drill. And every time you try to screw in something without a pilot hole because you don't feel like changing the bit on your cordless drill again and then spending ten minutes trying to get the screw to bite into the wood on its own, you can use a Yankee drill.

You can use your Yankee drill for standard drilling as well, and it is great for areas where you don't want to bring your heavier cordless drill. But just for drilling pilot holes alone, this gem will pay for itself the first few times you use it and you'll end up using it more than you expect.

Yankee drills are usually easier to find online than they are in hardware stores. They come with double-fluted bits—which work differently from the modern-style bits because they cut as you push and clear as you release. A good Yankee drill will run you about thirty bucks.

You won't regret getting one of these.

Narcissus

For a few months, in 1985, my roommate Kirk and I were in Boston. Starving. Well, probably not *medically* starving; we did have the olives and slices of lemons that we stole from the garnish tray of the bar where we were working. Altogether, I'd say we ate a real meal every two or three days.

When we first arrived in Beantown, we were eating pretty regularly. This was partially because of the fact that the YMCA on Huntington Avenue gave you a breakfast voucher for its cafeteria every day: one egg (any style), toast, and coffee. So, every morning, with the thirty-five-dollar-a-day room that Kirk and I split at the Y, we ate. And it was a great beginning to the day. But you can only stay at the Y for two weeks, so we had to move on. Later, when breakfast was removed from the budget, we missed that voucher and actually taunted each other with the chant: "One egg (any style), toast, and coffee."

When we both left Oneonta, New York, my mom had given us shoeboxes of food at the Greyhound bus station—oh, man, they were long gone: ham sandwiches on croissants, plastic jugs of Kool-Aid (frozen to keep them cold longer), apples, crackers, pepperoni, boiled eggs, cottage cheese containers filled with macaroni salad. All gone.

It had been my idea to leave Oneonta. I admit it. But it was Kirk's idea to go to Boston.

"I'm taking off," I said one day as I looked out of his apartment window that looked down on Market Street in Oneonta. "Come with me."

"To Binghamton? Why?"

"Because there's nothing for me here and there's nothing for you, either. C'mon, it'll be a blast."

And I made it sound like the beginning of a film—as if we were two desperadoes, two beaten men who would head out to make their fortunes and leave the place that had mocked them behind.

Me? I was nursing a seriously broken heart and damaged ego and didn't want to be around when school started back up again. And Kirk had flunked out last semester and couldn't reenroll until the spring semester anyway.

"I'm taking a semester off. I'm leaving. So come with me."

"Maybe," Kirk said as he flipped the channels until he got to an episode of *M*A*S*H*. "But not to Binghamton. If we're gonna go, let's *go*."

We toyed around with different locales: Chicago, Miami, we even thought of LA. But once we landed on the idea of Boston, Kirk was sure it was the place for us.

"Boston?" I asked.

"Yup. That's where we need to go."

So, Boston it was.

We took the seven-hour bus ride from Oneonta to Boston to scope everything out—to see how difficult jobs and apartments were to find. By midmorning of the very first day in town, at our very first interview, we both walked out with jobs in our pockets—and not just any jobs: For two college kids from the sticks, they were dream jobs, at Narcissus.

Kenmore Square is the intersection of Beacon Street and Commonwealth Avenue and was the heart of Boston nightlife. It was behind Fenway Park and Boston University, and the nightclub Narcissus was a huge place where students from both Harvard and Boston University came to spend their parents' money.

And Kirk and I were hired to be two of their newest employees.

The place was huge and actually held three clubs in one: Narcissus, Celebration, and Lipstick. But Narcissus was the gleaming, Studio 54–style jewel of the crown.

Because it happened so quickly, Kirk and I went to the club that night to see if the crowds really did bring pockets full of tips for their favorite bartenders, as we had been promised. And they did.

"Well, my friend," Kirk said as he clinked his beer glass against mine and screamed over the sound of a thousand college kids. "We are gonna be rich."

We were ecstatic. And as soon as we got back to Oneonta after our scouting mission, we began tossing everything we owned into a few bags and making plans for the jump to Boston.

Finding an apartment was the first challenge. With all the fees added up, between first and last months' rent and the security deposit, we would need to come up with thirty-two hundred dollars. Which we didn't have.

When we started working at Narcissus, we were earning a little bit of money, but the challenge was that there was a pecking order there and we had not earned the plum bartending slots yet. Because we worked during the day, we were scheduled for a lot of corporate parties and band things where we worked the service bar and our tips came from the waitresses who were supposed to give us a percentage. They never did.

And because there were so many bartenders at Narcissus, if we worked a night, Kirk and I would come home with thirty-five to forty-five dollars each—hardly the hundred bucks a night we had been hoping for. The good news was that the work was easy.

Unfortunately, what money we were earning was going straight to Terry, our very moody landlord—or whatever you want to call the person who ran the weekly hotel-style place where we were staying. Terry would wait behind his door, in the building where we lived, waiting for us to walk by. Then he would pop out like a sentry as soon as our feet hit the wooden landing.

"Well?" Terry scratched his chest through his Talking Heads T-shirt and held out his hand—like we had tried to sneak out of a window a thousand times before this. Without a word, we'd hand over the rent, forty bucks a night—or however close we could get to it. If Kirk and I were both working that night, our combined tips would equal forty, with a few bucks to spare. But if just one of us was on, we'd come up short, unless we had saved from a night when we both did work.

Forty dollars would get rid of Terry until the next day. Giving Terry only thirty-five dollars would lead to a tirade on how he wasn't a bank and we were the most worthless rags he'd ever met.

I don't know if *rags* was a Terry term or a Boston one; he was the only person we ever heard use it, and he did so often.

By October, we knew we had lost a lot of weight—each time we got dressed, it seemed like we had shrunk another pants size—but when the junkies on Washington Street took interest in our new, ultra-thin frames (probably thinking we might have a connection or a hit to share), we knew that food needed to become a bigger priority in our lives.

That's why the envelope was such a big deal.

Kirk found the envelope—and I can still see it after all these years—on High Street. It was in the shape of a small paper rectangle and had Asian lettering on it, and because we were pretty close to Chinatown, this made sense. Inside the envelope was a bright, red-foiled liner and a small card. The card had more lettering—stuff we couldn't read—but inside the card, pressed between the thick paper folds, were two crisp ten-dollar bills.

Kirk kept punching my shoulder. "We could have walked by it," he said, and he continued to punch me all the way to a Burger King, where we ordered two Whopper meals. We dove into the burgers and could only finish about half before our shrunken stomachs gave up.

"I know what's for dinner," Kirk said with a smile, as he wrapped his leftover sandwich back into the foil. We sat there for a long time, happy. Happy because not only did we have a meal, but we actually had the next one covered, too.

With the remaining money, we bought crackers, peanut butter, and beef jerky—stuff we could easily hide from Terry, because food in the room was forbidden and he checked regularly.

We had a certain routine, Kirk and I. Northeastern University had bought a huge apartment building near us and was converting it to dorms. We went exploring one day and found that the laundry room was never locked and within the room was an ironing board and iron. So, every day that we had to work, we would stop there and iron our black pants and white shirts before getting on the train to Kenmore Square—we didn't have an iron of our own and had been yelled at a few times for coming in with wrinkled clothes.

There was this very cute girl in the dorms with red hair we would see every now and then. She never paid much attention to us, but when Kirk went alone to iron his clothes, he would always come back telling me how she stopped to talk to him an flirt. But when we went back together, she ignored us again. Kirk was like that. On nights I didn't work, he would come back with stories of how the owners of the club would buy him shots and pretty bartenders would hit on him. But when we worked together, we were both invisible.

That's why I know the shooting probably didn't happen. Looking back, I guess it doesn't really matter whether it did or not, but it's most likely that Kirk made it up.

It was the second week of November and I was off for the night but Kirk was working. He came home excited. He told me a story about how there had been a robbery at the club and some guy had shot one of the bartenders. Then the shooter came back behind the bar, robbed the cash register, and headed out—only to be shot by cops before he made it to the street.

Like I said, the shooting probably didn't happen. But I never had a chance to verify it. It was the excuse I needed. I was going back to New York.

Kirk was sitting in the chair by the door as I threw my clothes into a bag. He looked at me with a mixture of fear and pain as I said good-bye. From Brookline, Massachusetts, I walked to the bus station where I used my last twenty-two dollars—my half of tomorrow's rent—to buy a ticket to Schenectady, where a friend picked me up and drove me the remaining two hours to my parents' house.

I left Kirk back in Boston, alone and broke in a city that didn't want him.

There are two kinds of bad decisions: mistakes and regrets.

A mistake is a miscalculation. An error. Bad data and bad calculations.

But a regret is when a moral or ethical line has been crossed, when you have the chance to do the right thing and you don't. Most regrets come from the wrong answer to one simple question: Do I stick or do I run?

A life filled with mistakes is not a bad life at all. It's one of excitement and energy and fire. But one filled with regrets will weigh you down because regrets don't have shelf lives and their backup batteries never run dry.

I never saw Kirk again. I have no idea what happened to him. I transferred to Cortland University the next semester. I do know that he didn't have any family—his mom had died when he was young and his father a few years after Kirk graduated high school.

So, here is the question: How hard would it have been to get us both to my parents' house? To get us both someplace safe until we figured out the next step? I never even asked Kirk if he wanted to go with me. How difficult would it have been to have thought about my friend even a fraction of the amount that I thought about myself?

Probably not very. It most likely would have taken the same amount of energy as it took to leave him behind.

Narcissus was the Greek god of self-love, and that coincidence isn't wasted on me. Neither is the fact that I have very few good memories of Boston—most likely because, in my mind, it represents the ugly parts of myself that I would prefer to forget. But I would like to think that if this same situation happened today, thirty years later, the man I am now would react differently and would show just a little bit of loyalty and grace.

I'd like to think so. But I'll never know for sure.

That's why they call them regrets.

How to Make the World's Greatest Venison Roast Recipe—Ever

The first thing I need to mention is, I don't hunt. Not at all.

And that's not because I'm against hunting; I'm not. I don't view hunting as wrong, cruel, or barbaric; in fact, as long as the meat is being used, I think it's a self-sufficient and admirable thing to do.

I grew up in a little town in the Catskill Mountains called Walton, New York. Although it might be different now, in those days, if Dad didn't get a deer, it was going to be a long winter. There were many families back then that depended on wild game to supplement their food stocks and the state police had a long list of families that would take deer killed in car accidents so the meat didn't go to waste.

I have no problem with hunting. Never did. I just don't hunt.

But all of us—myself included—know people who *do* hunt. Plenty of them. And hunters tend to be very generous people who enjoy sharing some meat with friends and family who will use it.

Which means, if you're like me and don't deer hunt, you still need to be familiar with how to cook venison, especially a venison roast. And the reason to focus on the roast is that, besides being a great piece of meat, it's not as sexy and sought after as, say, the tenderloin, which everyone prizes. So, many folks will have an extra venison roast in their freezer and are more than happy to share with all us nonhunters out there who enjoy it and know how to prepare it.

If you have family or friends who have never had venison and are a little apprehensive to try it—this is the recipe for you. That's actually how I came to get it.

My mother-in-law grew up as one of those people unfamiliar with venison, but *her* mother-in-law would cook it occasionally for Sunday dinner. This young, recently married woman did not want to insult her husband's mother, so she tried it. And she was hooked. The meat was tender, moist, and tasted . . . well, nothing like what she expected deer to taste like.

And that is this recipe here: the actual venison roast recipe from my wife's grandmother, Elsie Wilkins, circa 1950. It's the greatest venison roast recipe you will ever find and the only one you will ever need.

It's simple, fun to make, and has an amazing flavor.

Ingredients:

A 4- to 6-pound venison roast
Flour
1 tablespoon cooking oil
1 large onion
Half a head of garlic
4 teaspoons dried oregano
1 pinch celery seed
4 tablespoons wine vinegar (not cider vinegar)
Salt and pepper to taste
Accent™ to taste (Now, for all of you under forty, you may not know this brand name, and yes, it is high in sodium. But

it's how the original recipe was written, the product is still available, and it's what I suggest you use.)

Directions:

1. Peel half a head of garlic.

2. Cut small slits in the roast and place long pieces of garlic into the roast—this will add moisture while the roast is cooking.

3. Place the oil in the bottom of a French oven (a French oven is an enamel-covered version of a Dutch oven and retains heat a little better than its Dutch cousin) and bring up to medium heat on the stovetop.

4. Brown roast in oil for 10 to 15 minutes, or until you get a nice brown sear on all the edges.

5. Slice one large onion in half-moons and set aside.

6. Remove roast. Place onion and vinegar in French oven.

7. Rub spices liberally over the roast (Accent™, celery seed, salt and pepper, oregano).

8. Place roast on top of the onions and cook at 325 degrees for 3 to 4 hours.

9. Check halfway through to see if additional moisture is needed. There should be some liquid in the bottom; if not, add some.

And that's it.

Now, venison roast is one of those strange foods that you either love or hate. It's like liver and onions or softshell crab. Most people who were raised on venison have fond memories of it. But having tasted many different recipes for venison, I believe this one has one clear advantage. If you make Debbie's grandmother's venison roast and you don't like it, then you know: You don't like venison.

And that's one less thing you have to worry about.

Becoming the Nonpassive Person

There is this very strange, very weird, and very interesting social phenomenon that occurs when people encounter a stranger.

Here's the scenario:

You are stopping at a store on your way home from work. You locate the store and drive into the lot. You park and turn the car off. You step out of the car, close the door, and hit that little button on your key fob to lock the doors: click and beep. The car is safe.

You head toward the store, but as you are walking, you notice that someone is walking out of the store toward you. Unbeknownst to you, some incredibly fast and complicated mental calculations are being made, deep inside your brain—and most of them you won't even be aware of.

Within milliseconds, your subconscious sends out a probe to determine if the stranger's path will be beyond your personal space—in other words, will he be three feet away or more, which would place him outside of the danger zone? The probe comes back and the determination isn't good. At the current rate of speed and the space available between the parked cars, the stranger will walk within three feet of you.

A full second later, we move into prep mode, and this is when we first notice that something is occurring. We see the stranger and we begin to feel just the smallest amount of discomfort—just a tiny bit of unease. We continue walking. We get within four feet of the stranger and he looks up. We look up. Something clicks and we give the stranger—the look.

At this point, we state our greeting—this could be a "'sup?", "How ya doin'?", "Hey." The stranger responds, passes, and we continue to the store. Moment over.

Now, what just happened?

Well, a lot. We just gave the stranger the look, and the look is actually a big deal. To describe the look is fairly easy—and once you've noticed it, you'll see it all the time. It's simply this: If you press your lips together tightly—as tightly as you can—and smile. That's it. That's the look.

Why is it important? Well, what's interesting about the look is that it's the "Please don't hurt me" expression. It's the default passive reaction. It's the "I don't want any trouble, I'm just walking here" plea. It's the human equivalent of lying down to expose our belly to let the bigger dog—the important dog—know that we admit we are smaller and weaker. Yup, all that in one expression.

Why do we do this? And why do we care if we do?

Well, in the animal world there are two states: dominant and submissive. A submissive dog—a good dog—will show the dominant dog—the important dog—that it poses no threat. That they don't want to take anything from them. That they know their place.

But we are not dogs. We are people.

And that's where the trick lies, because when we were kids, we saw adults. We admired them and we developed this image—this often unrealistic, unobtainable, two-dimensional image—and we told ourselves that when we became adults we would be just as strong, just as sure, and just as smart as those around us.

Then we got older. And we were absolutely none of these things. We were frightened and unsure and confused and afraid. And because we knew these were not the traits of the men we saw, we determined that we weren't men. We had failed. Oh, sure, we might be a good person or a kind friend or a good son, but as men we had failed.

But we didn't.

Our parents—our grandparents, our bosses, our neighbors, all those men we saw as the ideal—were just as weak and just as afraid and just as stupid as we are. They weren't always strong and smart and selfless, and sometimes they did really dumb things.

We can be confident in our career and in our family. We can be satisfied with our home and with our finances. We can be in great physical shape and be a good father, a great husband, and a solid friend, but when it comes to ranking where we believe we fit on the "man chart," we will always, always, always rank ourselves lowly.

And that's because the chart is wrong. And every time we use the look, it pushes us down a tiny microscopic step. The stranger in the grocery-store parking lot we pass on the way in to the store is almost certainly not going to punch us as we pass by. We know that. But every time we use the look, we have internally just filed the moment away as if we had, in fact, run from a fight.

Being courteous is something we give.

Being passive is something that is taken from us, something that is done to us.

Because we are not the good dog. And we are not seven years old on a playground. We are strong, thinking people. And there is no place for being passive when you are a strong, thinking person. We either screw up or we don't. We go or we stay. We decide (and we will probably decide wrong), and we do it.

We are civil.
We are reasonable.
We are tolerant.
We are rational.
But we are not passive.

Skill #334:

How to Build a Workbench

One of the great ironies of tools and their use is that the absolute best area to work is on a workbench—a high, solid, well-lit structure on which to cut and use a vise and connect and create. No question. But in order to have the right workbench for you, you need to build one. And in order to build one, you'll need a workbench.

Well . . . this isn't completely true. You can build a workbench without one. But later on, when you're using the bench and you have it exactly the way you like it, you'll realize that it would have been so much easier to build it if you had had it before.

Now, in this world of mass-produced everything, why would you want to build your own workbench? Great question.

There are about a zillion reasons why. Well, that's not true, either. There are five, but they are five pretty good reasons:

Quality. Most workbenches are cheap, mass-produced structures. You can get workbenches and workbench kits, where you add your own lumber, everywhere from Lowe's to CVS—yup, I have seen workbenches for sale at CVS around Father's Day. Ninety percent of these benches are light, poorly designed structures that will not work well with your home, garage, or the type of projects you will be working on. But even the remaining ten percent that are fairly well designed and constructed were not designed specifically with you and your needs in mind.

Cost. For a fraction of the cost of the most expensive prebuilt workbench out there, you can build one yourself—actually, less than that. You can get a high-end workbench for almost a thousand dollars, and the lumber to build it on your own would cost around a hundred dollars.

Designed specifically for you. What type of work are you going to be doing and how do you like to do it? A workbench for wood carving is going to be different from one used to repair old radios. Are there enough outlets? Is there a place for your coffeepot and all the stuff you like to have around you while you work? By building it yourself you can make sure it is exactly the way you want it.

Designed specifically for your location. There are many times when you could find the ultimate prebuilt workbench—if your garage were bigger. Or your basement had more light. Or you had more space in the shed. You need to design your workbench for the real estate it will take up.

Sense of pride. There is something about building—well, building anything—that pays an emotional dividend. But there is great irony in having a structure to build things on that you didn't build.

So, how do you build a workbench? Here are a few things to consider.

Location. Decide where the bench will go. This is actually more important than the design of the bench itself. Examine the area where it will be, looking all around: Is there enough light, enough storage space? Is it easy to get materials in and out? A workbench for finally building that canoe you've dreamed of may not work well in your basement, where you can't get the finished product back out.

Overall design. There are some great sites online that offer workbench plans and a quick web search will help you find many of them. Choose an overall plan and then look at the areas you want to personalize, such as the height of the bench. If you don't like any of the plans, just draw what you do like and add in the two important aspects: power and light. You will want to attach at least one strip right to the workbench for power and you'll need at least one flexible lamp for additional light.

Simpson ties. If there is one magic trick when it comes to building a solid, rugged workbench, it's Simpson ties—a fancy name for metal pieces that attach to wood to strengthen it. Look at any shed or wooden building and in the corner, you will see the shiny metal Simpson ties. And because a workbench is not a table but rather a heavy-duty work structure that you can use to put something in a vise, saw, or hammer, you want it to be solid. By using Simpson ties for the corners of your bench and where the lumber fits together, your bench will be rock solid.

Overdesign for material. As with any project, once you finalize your design and make your materials list, add about twenty-five percent more of everything you think you'll need. This is a handyman trick that works, because it is far better to make one trip back to Lowe's when you're done to return what you didn't use than it is to make six extra trips for what you forgot.

Take your time. As you get going, you may want to make changes or add in new pieces of jewelry to the project. No rush. Take your time.

Building your own workbench isn't a necessity, but it does pay off because buying something usually comes with very little pride attached—maybe the temporary kind. But there is always pride in building something. It's the bonus that comes with the blisters.

Riley the Dog

There are a few things in my household that I have complete veto power over—not many, but there are a handful. For example, when my wife and children wanted pets, I said no. I felt bad about it, but the answer was no. I did not want us to be one of those "pet houses."

Now, don't get me wrong, pets are great: cute, fun, entertaining—I get it. But having animals means being tied down, constantly running home and feeding them or letting them out or exercising them. I wanted us to be able to travel and move around freely without having to be animal caretakers.

So, I said no. No pets.

And to their credit, my family reacted in a way that made me proud. There were no complaints from Debbie and no tears from the kids. They all took it extremely well.

And one morning—this would have been about three years later—I was feeding the cats when Debbie and the kids said that they wanted a dog.

What? A dog? No, absolutely not. No dogs.

And they took it well.

Then then, about three years later, when they asked for *another* dog? Absolutely not. *We already had a dog.*

But they said a new dog would be a companion to Abby, our golden retriever. And, they added, a second dog is not much more work than a first dog. Once again, I pulled out my veto power and said no. Sorry, but no. We would not be a house with two dogs—who has two dogs anyway? That's like having two swimming pools or two basements. Why would you have more than one?

And five years later, after Murphy died, we were back to only one dog, so . . .

Well, you get the picture.

So we got Riley.

The difference between Riley and the other dogs we've had—two golden retrievers and a basset hound—is that Riley is a mixed-breed dog.

After having had three purebreds I have realized that all breeds are bred to do something—to hunt, to point, to herd, to show, to . . . something. And their DNA is telling them to herd, to protect, to point—first. Then, if they have some free time left over, they can be a pet.

Now, many breeds make excellent pets—it says so right in the book—but some are first and foremost bred to do something else.

Not that purebred dogs aren't great. They are. But I prefer my mutt.

When you take out that breeding—rip out the generations of DNA that force a dog to react a certain way or be on the lookout for a specific action and strip the dog down to its basic structure—you let the dog just be a dog.

And when you get to be just a dog, you have the opportunity to see the world through a regular ol' dog's eyes. And frankly, dogs have it all figured out. Riley has it all figured out.

So, here is what Riley has to tell you about life:

Where you are is the place to be.
Riley doesn't wonder if there is something better upstairs or around the corner. All he knows is that right here, right now,

is where it's at. This is the center of the universe and where he's happy and grateful. He doesn't regret or second-guess. This moment, this time, is the best time that there is or will ever be.

All memories are good memories.

Riley doesn't mentally file away the times you bumped his nose when walking past him in the middle of the kitchen. He forgot how Abby got three more dog biscuits than he did and he has no clue that you could have walked him an hour earlier on Sunday but chose not to. Riley doesn't know how to keep memories like this or what to do with them even if he did. He doesn't understand what envy or jealousy or bitterness is, and if he did, he would abandon it. It would bore him.

As great as life is, there is always room for new people.

Riley loves the people around him and is content with just them, forever. But when a new person enters his life, he reacts as if this is the first person he has ever met. Riley doesn't treat his tenth friend as in any way less than his first friend. Everyone who enters his world is amazing, valuable, and worth getting to know. And he does not respond to people based on how they respond to him. He doesn't care. He focuses on them, regardless of what they think about him.

And that's what Riley wanted me to tell you.

Skill #251:

How to Jumpstart a Car

The basics of jumpstarting a car are extremely simple and require only three parts: one, a car with a dead battery—the "jumpee;" two, a car with a live battery—the "jumper;" and three, a set of large, industrial jumper cables.

Now, this is a very simple process that can get complicated quickly if you have undersized jumper cables—or lack cables entirely. The reason for this is that it's always easier to find someone willing to give your car a jumpstart than it is to find someone who is both willing to do so and also happens to have a set of jumper cables—or a set large enough to actually work. You may find one or you may find the other, but you need to find both. It's kind of like needing help moving, but only being allowed to accept help from friends with red hair or those who are left-handed—you've not only decreased your odds, but you've put yourself in a vulnerable position.

Being car owners means that we have to be prepared to take care of ourselves, the people we care about, and others who may need our help along the way.

It's okay to have a dead battery. It's not okay to drive around unprepared, expecting others to take care of us. A guy on the side of the road with a sign reading NEED JUMPER CABLES is different from the man with his hood up, cables ready, looking for a quick charge from a passing traveler.

And don't think for one minute that those cheap jumper cables that came with the car or the ones in the emergency kit your aunt gave you for Christmas count. They don't. They are worthless and unreliable. I have had to stop to help more people who were trying to jumpstart with cheap cables than people who had no cables at all. Those lousy cables just don't work. Go out and get yourself a heavy set of jumper cables—six-gauge or better (the lower the gauge number, the better, so six is better than eight and four is better than six, and so on), three-hundred-amp or better cables with rubber handles on the clamps—not plastic ones. Fifteen feet is a good length. Twelve-foot cables are often hard to use if you have to pull the cars in at a strange angle, and with more than fifteen feet, you risk some current loss.

Here's the process:

Now, let's say you've got a decent set of jumper cables, a car that needs to be jumpstarted (the jumpee), and a car that is has a fully charged battery (the jumper). From here, it's pretty straightforward. With the jumper's car running—it's very important that the car doing the jumpstarting is running—you'll start the process.

First, you need to determine if the problem with the car truly is a dead battery. If, when you turn the key, the car does nothing or if it tries to turn over but can't, it's most likely the battery. If the dash lights come on and/or there is a clicking sound when you try to start the car, this might be a starter issue instead of a battery.

Many people believe that it doesn't matter which way you connect the cables, as long as they are the same on both cars. However, the positive, or red, cable is actually slightly larger than the negative cable. So, the cables were designed to connect red to positive and black to negative.

So, you connect the red jumper cable clamp to the positive terminal on the jumpee car, then the red jumper cable clamp to the positive terminal on the jumper. Next, you'll go back and connect the black to negative on the jumpee and then black to the heavy metal bracket of the battery or frame of the jumper.

Wait a minute to let a charge build up, then try to start the jumpee car. If it starts, great. If it doesn't, wait a few more minutes and let the charge build up further. Try again. If nothing happens, look at the cars you are matching up.

If you have a Honda Civic and you're trying to jumpstart a Chevy Bronco, you may have an issue. The smaller battery may not be strong enough to charge the larger one. You can wait a bit longer to see if a charge will build, but most likely you will need to find a larger car to jump from. You want the battery of the jumper to be equal to or larger than that of the jumpee.

If this is not the case, if you are stranded along the road and the only car that is available to help jumpstart your Ford F150 is a Nissan Stanza, you can allow the charge to build and give it a few minutes with the cables connected to build up a charge. But it will depend on how dead the battery is.

But if the battery sizes are equal and the cables are of industrial strength, you should get a charge and the car should start. If so, unhook the cables—red from the jumper then red from the jumpee, and so forth—and let the car run to build up a charge.

That's it.

So, now do you know how to jumpstart a car?

No. Because you haven't done it yet.

Put a good set of cables in your trunk and wait to find someone you can help. Once you've actually jumpstarted a car, then you can say for sure that know how to do it.

And when you find someone—as you walk out with your heavy-duty cables still in their plastic bag—be honest.

Tell the person that you have never used the cables but you're willing to try to help.

Don't be embarrassed. I found my neighbor—he was almost sixty at the time—reading his car manual trying to figure out how to jumpstart his car. He refused to let me help him because he didn't want to admit that he didn't know how to do it.

And knowledge that is offered but not accepted is wasted knowledge. And that's the worst kind.

Clara

When my son Alex was about ten years old, we saw Clara for the first time. We were in the car, we had just turned off Fiddlers Green and onto Governors Avenue, and there she was, over to the left side of the road, coming toward us.

It was cold outside and Clara was pushing her grocery cart against traffic, the way bicyclists do, and the wheels of the cart were biting into the gray slush of the road. Alex saw her and stopped talking. We drove another hundred yards or so before he spoke again.

"We've got to go back," he said.

Now, I know I saw Clara—not really acknowledging her, but seeing her the same way I saw the Burger King sign and the Michelin store behind her. But Alex had locked in on her. He really *saw* her.

"We've got to go back," he repeated.

"Why?"

Alex told me what he'd seen: that there was an old woman in the street. Everything she owned was in one grocery cart and it was cold outside. We had to go back. To help.

"Great idea," I said magnanimously, as I mentally inventoried what cash I had on me—hoping I had something smaller than a twenty.

"No," he corrected me. "We need to take her—home. To our house. To live."

We kept driving and I told Alex how proud I was of him. I praised the great heart he had and told him what a great kid he was. And then I gently explained how we could help. With a little bit of money.

"No," he said. "We need to take her home with us."

I explained all the reasons why we couldn't do that. The lady was a stranger. We couldn't bring a stranger into our house; it wasn't safe. We could help, sure, a little, but we ...

Alex looked at me with focused eyes. "But, Dad, she's old. And it's cold, and we have that big guest room that no one is using and she can ..."

He kept talking and we kept driving. When we got to Walmart, he was still talking—well, I was still talking. Alex was anxiously trying to hurry us up, to get us back in the car and rolling toward Governors Avenue.

"How about we get her some food while we're here, huh? How about that?" I suggested.

"No," he said.

But I did it anyway. I picked out a few prepackaged sub sandwiches, some chips, and some bottled water and I listened to Alex plead. As I did, I understood that he didn't want to bring this woman home the way you do a kitten or a lost dog. He wanted her to come home with us to become part of us. To be a member of our family.

Why? It was simple. We had the space. We had a house that was warm and dry and there was plenty of food there. In his view, there was no reason to discuss it any further. We had resources that someone else didn't. It was only fair.

We drove back to Governors Avenue, to the place we had seen her, and she was gone. We drove farther down, through the side streets. Nothing. We looked inside Burger King and at the bus stop and then circled the entire loop again, but we couldn't find her.

"Okay," I said. "I have an idea."

Alex looked up at me as if there was nothing I could have done to disappoint him more. We pulled into the homeless shelter that was on Governors Avenue and I parked the car. We walked inside and told the lady at the desk who we were and who we had had seen and that we wanted to get this food to her.

The woman knew exactly who I was referring to and told us her name was Clara.

Clara had been in and out of the shelter many times. She had been offered job opportunities and even an apartment, but something always happened. The woman at the desk told Alex how proud she was of him for wanting to take Clara home. But she explained that we had to be safe and that there were other ways to help.

And Alex, silent, looked up at the both of us with frustrated eyes. We could show him statistics, photographs, evidence all day long and it wouldn't matter. Here were the only facts that did: There was a woman who needed help. We were able to help. Done.

We left the food at the shelter—the woman at the desk didn't know if Clara would be in, but she promised she would make sure it went to good use—and then we walked back out to the car.

"Feel better?" I asked.

"No." And he didn't.

We saw Clara a few more times after that. And then we didn't see her again.

Alex is in his twenties now. And he still has a gentle heart and is a sensitive, caring kid. But he has a filter now about things like this. The same kind of filter we all have.

Now, there was no way that Clara could have come home to live with us. Absolutely not. I wouldn't jeopardize the safety of my family, I know that. Everyone knows that. It never would have happened.

But still. There's something so . . . so absolutely pure about putting what we *should* do ahead of what we *can* do. And instead of finding a way to nurture that better sentiment in Alex, I somewhat yanked it out of him.

And I feel bad about that.

Loctite and J-B Weld— How to Choose the Right Product for the Right Job

On the pegboard behind my workbench hang some very cool tools. There are coping saws, drills, laser levels, a miter box—well, to get technical, the miter box actually sits on a shelf below, but I just like saying "miter box"—and a bunch of other cool stuff.

Most of these tools I've used—some not so often and a few not at all, but each of them looks amazing hanging there. In fact, sometimes I go down in the basement and just visit my tools, admiring them like a painting.

Now, it's not that I'm afraid of these tools or that I just wanted to collect them. The truth is that ninety percent of the time when I do something around the house, I don't need much in the way of tools. I don't do major construction; I just like to putz around the house, tinker with some things, make repairs and small upgrades when needed. So, the majority of work I do could be completed with only five items.

In fact, if I had to keep only five objects from my workbench and use only them, I'd be pretty safe by keeping:

:: A roll of duct tape;

:: A can of WD-40;

:: A cheap, multihead screwdriver;

:: A pair of needle-nose pliers; and

:: Loctite (the greatest glue ever) and J-B Weld (a two-tube product that, when mixed, becomes as hard as metal).

Boom.

That would get me—as well as the majority of people—through most of the quick fixes and minor repairs that need to be done around the home.

There are many tools that can do many things. It's like brand names: Eighty percent of the time, brand names are not that important—you get the same result from Brand B as you would from Brand A—but twenty percent of the time, when the brand name is important, it's really important. Which brings me to a crucial brand-name difference when it comes to a superglue like Loctite.

First, make sure it's Loctite. If you think that by Loctite, I'm referring to generic superglue, you are incorrect. Next to GPS and luggage with wheels, Loctite—the real superglue—is one of the greatest inventions in the past hundred years. It can be used for everything from sealing a cut to repairing coffee mugs to being mixed with baking soda and used like caulk.

Although Loctite might have invented superglue, not all superglue is Loctite. This may seem like a minor point, but it's not. In fact, the next time you are standing at Walmart, looking at the superglue, the crazy glue, and the super bondo, if you don't see the Loctite brand, just walk away.

Loctite was developed in the 1950s as a thread-locking adhesive. The formula worked so well that the company developed other glues, and Loctite was the industrial staple for decades. Simply put, when you buy Loctite, you know it is going to work. Any glue can add the word *super* or *crazy* to its name and still be just glue. Why take the chance that another brand might not work when you know that Loctite is a liquid weld?

There are, however, those occasions when Loctite just doesn't have the firepower you need. And that's where J-B Weld comes in.

J-B Weld is an inexpensive product that comes in two small tubes. When you mix the contents of these two tubes together, a chemical reaction occurs, and you get a liquid that, when hardened, becomes stronger than metal.

J-B Weld is amazing and can be used on everything from repairing fuel tanks to patching bathtubs to welding pipes.

You can find J-B Weld in any hardware store or auto parts store. It costs about five bucks and pays for itself with the first use. I used it recently to repair a fireplace screen that was in five pieces and ready for the dumpster. That one pack saved me over two hundred bucks, and you use such a small amount of it that a single pack will last years.

J-B Weld is a cold-weld process. The product comes in two toothpaste-type containers. One will have a white product and the other will be black. On a piece of cardboard, you dab equal amounts next to each other, then mix them together until they are a gray color. There is an odd, fishy smell when you first mix the substances, but it doesn't last long. Once mixed, you apply with a small brush and wait.

The downside to J-B Weld is that it takes several hours to harden—in some thick applications, I've gone back ten hours later and it was still slightly tacky. The good news is that when it does harden, it's there forever. You can even sand

and drill through it, if necessary—like I said, they repair gas tanks with this stuff.

So, spend the seven bucks and get a bottle of Loctite and a pack of J-B Weld and you'll be all set.

And then you can use the money you saved to buy gas to drive over to my place and admire all my tools with me.

The Broken Gauge

From the moment we are born, when we are a minute old, right to the day before our eighteenth birthday, we fall under a specific legal category: We are minors.

Now, the dictionary definition of *minor* is "of lesser in importance, seriousness, or significance." As minors, we cannot vote or buy tobacco, we cannot serve in the military, and we cannot make legal decisions on our own.

But at eighteen years of age, this changes. We leave the state of "minorship" and enter adulthood. This is the line. There are the things that happened before we are eighteen— during our childhood—and then everything that occurs after—when we are adults.

There is no clear reason why eighteen was chosen for the age of adulthood. Many historians will say that it is tied to the age of students when they completed public school and began college enrollment. Whatever the case, an age had to be chosen and eighteen made sense.

So, before eighteen, we are minors.

At eighteen, we are adults.

By twenty-two, we should be done with college or have a career path chosen.

By twenty-five, we should be living completely independently and should be financially established.

By thirty, we should be married.

By thirty-five, we should have kids.

By forty, we should be hitting our career stride, making a good income and raising our children.

By forty-five, we should be upper management.

By fifty, we should be reaching our area of peak income potential.

By fifty-five, we should have our kids in a good college.

By sixty, we should be looking toward retirement and the good life.

This is the path.

This is the gauge against which we are expected to measure ourselves—and others. If we are ahead of the curve, then we are successful. If we are behind it, we are failing. And all of this is based on the fact that we are considered adults at eighteen. Eighteen is where it is supposed to all begin. This is when the grading starts.

But there are some serious flaws with this type of reasoning.

The biggest one is that the human brain—the device that has complete control over everything we think, reason, decide, and do—is still developing until the age of twenty-five. That's the reason why our car insurance rates don't begin to go down until the age of twenty-five: because it's not until that age that our brains are finally done "cooking" and can now think clearly.

So, at twenty-five, we finally have all the mental equipment we will ever be given. Unfortunately, according to the gauge, we should already be seven years into our path. And if we're not—if, at twenty-five or thirty, we are just starting to understand things—we are a failure. And worse, we have missed the boat. The opportunities have left us and we'll just have to get by some other way.

But this is absolutely not true.

Life decisions do not have expiration dates. If you started college and then stopped, you don't go *back* to college to finish; you go to college. You don't go *back* to your old profession that you started out in; you just decide that it's the industry in which you want to make a living.

Fifty is as good an age to begin a business as thirty is. Twenty is just as good a time to go to college as forty. And learning to play the guitar, speak Spanish, dive, or juggle has no age limit at all.

There is no "back."

The gauge is broken.

Skill #157:

How to Change a Tire

In 2011, *U.S. News and World Report* reviewed a study performed by AutoMD that looked at trends among new drivers. One of the most interesting discoveries the study uncovered was that two-thirds—over sixty percent—of all new drivers between the ages of sixteen and nineteen could not change a flat tire.

In fact, the study went on to state that the same percentage—over sixty percent—of these teen drivers were also unable to jumpstart a dead battery or even check their oil. This means two-thirds of us starting out in our driving careers are incapable of performing the most rudimentary maintenance tasks or making basic field repairs on our vehicles.

Now, this is not a truly shocking statistic—younger drivers aren't as experienced as more seasoned ones. So what? Younger drivers need to be able to develop skills such as changing a tire. But add that to my own personal study of the four dozen or so men I've stopped to help change tires. Half of them were older than I am and they still had no idea how to change a tire.

It's understandable. A skill such as changing a tire isn't one you can really practice. And in theory, if we replace our tires when they get worn and never hit a bottle or a nail, or never ride too hard over a curb, it's possible we might never need to change a tire at all.

It's always possible.

But why take a chance? If you know the basics, then you'll actually be able to change a tire without having to yank a tire off your car and practice a few times. If you understand the process, you'll be ready when it comes time to act on that knowledge.

So, how do you change a tire?

Get to a flat place or a safe place that will allow you to work on the tire. If you have to change a tire alongside a busy highway, this may be difficult. It's important to get your car as far away from traffic as possible, to a place that will give you space to jack up the car and work on it safely. Pull over or even ride the car on the rim if you need to until you find somewhere safe. I've seen guys on the side of the road trying to change a tire with their legs spread halfway into the road. The cost of a tow or a new wheel is a steal compared to the cost of your life. If it doesn't feel safe to change the tire yourself, don't do it. Call a tow truck.

Put the parking brake on. With an automatic transmission, put the parking brake on and leave it in park. If you have a manual transmission, put the parking brake on and leave the car in reverse as an extra precaution. You can also slide something under the front and back tires to prevent it from rolling.

Locate the spare tire. This may not be as easy as it sounds. Once upon a time, spare tires were stored in the trunk. Period. But many cars—such as hatchbacks and minivans—don't have trunks. In those cases, the spare tires are often mounted under the carpeting of the back or under the car itself, with a release under the mat in the car. When in doubt, consult the car's owner's manual.

When you do find the spare, don't be surprised if it is an emergency spare or "donut"—a small spare tire that is meant to get you to a garage and is only intended to be used for a limited number of miles. With the exception of large SUVs and trucks, few cars come equipped with a full-sized spare tire. Each donut spare is different, but they are usually only designed to be used for thirty to fifty miles.

Locate the tools. When you find the tire, you will most likely find a scissor jack and tire iron as well. If not, many cars have side compartments where the tools are kept.

Loosen the lug nuts—the nuts that hold the wheel to the axle. Many people think you jack the car off the ground and then start loosening the lug nuts. Nope. Doing that not only makes the lugs harder to loosen, but the shaking and moving of the car could make it unstable. Get the lug nuts loose— what is called "breaking the seal"—and then jack the car up. And don't be tricked by those fancy wheel covers that look like lug nuts. Check to see if there is a hubcap that has to be removed first.

Jack the car up. This may seem intimidating at first, but it's not. Get the jack under the frame near the tire that has to be changed. Most car frames will have a slot cut into them next to each tire where the top of the jack will fit perfectly. Place the jack directly under that notch and twist the lever to start opening the jack. Most scissor jacks allow you to insert the tire iron into a slot to be used as a handle. Start cranking. And remember, you don't need the car six feet off the ground. Getting the tire just a few inches off the ground is often enough. You can always adjust once you get the old tire off.

Remove the lug nuts. Use the tire iron and remove the nuts and set them aside.

Remove the old tire and replace it with spare tire. Once the spare is on, place the lug nuts back on and tighten them by hand. Then, you want to lower the car slightly so the spare is just touching the ground. This will allow you to tighten the lug nuts without the tire spinning.

Tighten the lug nuts in a star pattern. That is, tighten one slightly, then go to the one directly across from it, and repeat. Then tighten the one next to that, then the one across from that. Don't tighten one lug nut completely and then go on to the next. If you do, they will be tightened unevenly and the tire will wobble—or even come off while you're driving.

Drive the car to a shop and get a new tire put on.

The Art of the Used Suit

In the world of theater, television, and film, there is never enough credit given to the props department. These people are absolutely amazing. There is so much to this art and a great deal more than simply finding stuff and placing it in an actor's hand. There is some very serious psychology involved.

For example, if there's ever a scene where a character enters a home after grocery shopping, you'd think the props would be simple, right? A bag of groceries. So the props people will put together something called "standard urban groceries," or SUG. These are items that don't appear together in real life but when you see them on film or the stage, your mind will accept them.

They are the single brown-paper shopping bag, out of the top of which you will see a French baguette, the overflowing greens of a bunch of carrots, and the nondescript top of a carton of milk.

Standard urban groceries exist only in the TV world.

Suits are another thing that we accept on screen. A commercial with a dad coming home from work will always have him wearing a suit, with his tie undone. An airport will be full of men in suits hurrying to make connections, and the business conference room scene will have men in dark suits huddled around a shiny table with a view of a major metropolitan city behind them.

But in actuality, since the birth of business casual in the 1990s, very few American men wear suits to work—outside of the industries of medicine and law, there are very few professions that still embrace the suit. So, when dad comes home from a harried day, he will most likely be in khakis and a polo, not a suit.

The suit is not the day-to-day necessity it once was, but we still accept it as normal on film. And even if you don't have to wear a suit every day, it's still important to have a few in your closet. Besides the times when you will absolutely need a suit—weddings and funerals—by having a few suits, you will be more likely to choose one when you have the option: "I could wear a suit if I had one, but I'll just wear this instead."

So, get a few suits. And when buying suits, buy used.

Now, if you've never bought used clothing, get over it. If you don't ever buy any other item used, the suit is the one. First of all, suits are worn very infrequently, so the average suit has probably been worn only a handful of times— maybe even just once—and will have seen just a fraction of the wear that other used clothing has.

Because used suits are usually sold by condition rather than brand name, buying used can get you a much higher-quality suit than you could afford new. I've personally owned three Brooks Brothers suits in my life, and all were bought for under thirty bucks and then tailored. My son has a beautiful Perry Ellis suit that we bought for ten dollars and then spent sixty to have it tailored for him. So, for seventy dollars, he has a three-hundred-dollar suit that he uses several times a year.

Used suits will give you more options when it comes to different styles than you would see in a men's retail shop. For the same price as a suit at the mall, you can have three or four suits bought, tailored, dry-cleaned, and waiting in your closet.

When buying a used suit, there are a few guidelines you should follow:

Buy from a store. There are many online retailers that offer luxury used suits online. But unless you have already tried on that style of suit before, go to a store—you'll be able to try it on, plus you'll save on the shipping.

Stick to the basic places. Sure, there are designer used clothing stores, but these places offer you nothing more than the thrift stores do, and at higher prices. The places to shop are the Goodwill, church thrift stores, the Salvation Army, and the like—these places have racks and racks of suits and mark up on condition only. Depending on the part of the country you're in, a practically new suit should run you thirty dollars or less.

Buy tall. Because you are going to have the suit tailored anyway, choose a suit that fits, or is slightly bigger, at the shoulders and the waist and don't worry about sleeve and pant length. The easiest thing for a tailor to fix is the length of the pants and jacket sleeves. More difficult are the waist of the pants and the shoulders of the jacket—now, if you find the ultimate suit that is slightly big in these areas, I'm not saying not to get it. Just be prepared and know that your tailoring costs will go up slightly.

Get a few. Because you're buying used, get more than one suit. Your closet should have a dark blue suit, a dark gray, and then lighter gray or brown. For less than a hundred dollars at a thrift store, you can get a combination of three.

Get several ties. You should get three or four ties per suit to mix and match—and ties are another great thing to get a thrift store. There are millions of them, and usually they run around a dollar a piece.

Get it tailored. Don't try to save money by not getting the suit fitted. Even if it looks like it was made for you, spend the extra few bucks and have it tailored specifically to your body.

We all know that the value of a new car goes down as soon as the car leaves the lot. Well, the same is true with suits.

You could pick up a five-hundred-dollar Brooks Brothers suit that was worn once for thirty dollars. And thrift stores are loaded with used suits; the suit section is often the biggest area in the store, so there are a lot to choose from.

Used suits are an amazing overlooked resource. And although thrift-store people look for brands such as Rolex and Tiffany, they often don't pay attention to suit brands such as Boss and Christian Dior. To them, a suit is a suit.

Which is a bonus for you.

Skill #400:

How to Play the Harmonica

The harmonica—also known as the mouth organ or blues harp—is a great little instrument. In fact, the harmonica is the great equalizer of all musical instruments because you don't need to be able to read music to play one. You don't even need to have any true musical ability. It doesn't take years of dedication to master the harmonica. Actually, you can bang out a few tunes in just twenty minutes or so, and unlike the hundreds or thousands of dollars that many musical instruments cost, you can get a decent harmonica for about twenty bucks. Plus, a harmonica does not take up a great deal of space. I often carry mine in my shirt pocket.

Also, the harmonica has the distinction of being the only musical instrument I know of that you can play one-handed while driving. I am neither confirming nor denying that I have ever done this; I'm just saying it can be done.

And in the category of harmonica trivia, though I have no proof, it is very possible that a harmonica may have saved my life.

It was about ten years ago or so—I had a twelve-state sales territory back then—and I was driving through the great state of Texas when I saw a man hitchhiking. Now, hitchhikers were rare in my part of New York, so I decided to stop and give this traveler a ride—help out a stranger kind of thing—as well as swap a few stories. As I pulled over and the man started running toward me, I realized I might have made a mistake.

The guy was real rough—tattoos everywhere, including every knuckle—and several piercings, which really didn't concern me. What did send up some warning signals was the panicked expression on his face—the fact that he kept looking nervously behind him and the way his hands were shaking uncontrollably.

My instincts were screaming by the time he reached the car, but before I could think of a safe way to bow out of this arrangement, the man stuck his head in the passenger window and looked at me. Then he looked at the cup holder where my harmonica sat. Then he looked back at me. Then back to the harmonica. Then a moment of silence passed before he spoke.

"No, thanks," he said. And he walked away.

Just like that.

A few minutes later, I was back on Texas Route 273.

Now, I've always wondered what that hitchhiker thought when he saw my harmonica. Maybe his instincts were screaming as loud about me as mine were about him, or maybe he had never dealt with the kind of sociopath who would travel with a harmonica in his cup holder. But from that day on, I always keep a harmonica in the car and I am proud to say that I have never been murdered. Not even once.

Coincidence?

I don't think so.

So, how do you play the harmonica?

The harmonica is an instrument that creates different notes when you blow in from the notes it plays when you draw out. The key here is not to think of sucking and blowing, but just of breathing. Practice breathing in and out while playing the harmonica—play a few chords out, then draw back and breathe in.

For some reason, the song "Oh! Susanna" is the great beginner harmonica song. Practice breathing in and out on the harmonica while playing the song by ear. Focus on learning two things: notes and chords.

To play a single note on a harmonica, you just purse your lips so air blows through a single slot, making one note. To play a chord, you blow into that slot and the few around it. When you're first learning, focus on chords; that will give you a larger margin of error.

Once you can play the basic sounds of "Oh! Susanna," on chords, try playing it with single notes. This is a little more difficult than playing chords, but it will start to give you muscle memory on where the individual notes are.

And those are the bare bones on playing the harmonica. Pretty simple, huh? That's because the harmonica is one of those rare instruments that can easily be self-taught.

So, pick up a cheap harmonica today. You can get good ones at any music store for around ten bucks. Toss it in your pocket, your backpack, your tackle box, or if you are in West Texas, place it in the cup holder of your car.

You won't regret it.

The Heart of Cool

There is a supermarket near us where my wife, Debbie, often sends me to get last-minute items. It's a short drive from our house and is ideal when we need one green pepper or a dozen eggs, things like that. And yes, it's convenient. And yeah, it's reasonably priced. But more important, it's where a kid named Ethan works.

Now, I'm using the word *kid* here because I have no idea of Ethan's real age. He's young—but every year, a larger slice of the population looks young to me—and he does have those weird double earrings that appear as if dime-sized holes were drilled through his earlobes. If I had to guess, I'd say he was somewhere between seventeen and the ripe old age of twenty. Which, by using the age barometer that we middle-aged men carry, puts him well within the "kid" range.

The first time I met Ethan at the grocery store, he was loading yogurts in a dairy case. I walked right by him, to the next glass door. I had already looked in there for the frozen macaroni and cheese that Debbie sent me for, but you never know; maybe I missed what I wanted, so I looked again. Nope. And when I didn't find it for the second time, I closed the door, turned, and saw Ethan's half-smile.

"I look lost, huh?"

"Maybe," Ethan said with a smirk.

"I'm looking for the Bob Evans macaroni and cheese. You know, the ones that . . ."

It was then that Ethan's smirk became a wider smile.

"I gotcha," he said, nodding, as if in the history of food shopping, Bob Evans macaroni and cheese was the greatest thing that anyone had ever looked for. Ever. The look he gave me made me feel like only those like me—the rare, the connected, the exceptional—would even think to ask for Bob Evans macaroni and cheese.

Ethan abandoned his pallet of yogurts and walked me over three aisles. He then opened a refrigerator case to reveal two shelves of Bob Evans food products. There. Just waiting for me.

I thanked Ethan and he smiled and went back to his yogurt.

After that, anytime I couldn't find something, I would seek Ethan out—sure, I could have found it myself. Eventually. But even if I did, I would have missed out on that "cool" experience.

Because that's what Ethan is. He is one of those rare individuals who are just naturally cool. Not cocky. Not arrogant. Not proud, smug, or conceited. Cool—because there is a big difference.

And cool is so much better than all those other things. Cool is even better than just being confident and self-assured.

Because cool is . . . hey, it's cool.

Cool is the ability to be positive, but so much so that people feel confident around you. Cool is inviting. Cool is happy and content—it's the attitude that no matter where you are, that's the place to be.

Cool doesn't hide anything, but it celebrates everything. It can't be bought, it can't be faked, and it can't be forced. It's not a destination; it's a side effect.

Which means that if we try to get to cool, we never will. Ever. By trying, we'll get lost or we'll think we're there— which is much worse than not being cool at all.

Cool has nothing to do with what you wear, what you drive, how much money you make, who you know, or where you've been. Cool doesn't care about any of that.

And cool isn't perfect or flawless; cool makes mistakes and has errors and even regrets. But cool doesn't hide those mistakes; it celebrates them.

If you think you're cool, you're not. If you don't care if you're cool, you might be—but most likely, you're still not.

But whether or not we have the ability to be cool, we all have the ability to do things that are cool—which is almost as good.

Because every time we make someone feel important, powerful, or essential—that's cool.

Every time we ignore what is normal, standard, or average and embrace what simply feels right—that's cool.

Every time we turn the attention from us to someone else in a public way—that's cool.

Every time we enjoy something from the background, every act that is kind, every chance we have to step forward even though we're scared to death, every aspect of beauty that we notice that we've never seen before . . .

That's very, very cool.

How to Iron Clothes

There is nothing that screams, "Yes, yes, my mother did used to do my laundry" than when a man shows up wearing wrinkled clothes.

There is nothing that screams, "Yes, yes, an iron is way too heavy, complicated, frightening, and/or dangerous for me to operate" than when a man shows up wearing wrinkled clothes.

And there is nothing that screams, "Yes, yes, I have officially given up on what I look like and how others see me" more than when a man shows up wearing wrinkled clothes.

Nothing.

Ironing your own clothes is right above making your own meals and right below driving your own car. It's a basic, modern-day survival skill.

So learn it. Do it. Live it.

Now, we are discussing ironing, not laundry, but there is one important rule of laundry that will guide your ironing success. And it's this:

Don't use the dryer.

With the exception of socks, underwear, and blue jeans, never, ever dry your clothes in a dryer. Hang everything out to dry—not necessarily outdoors but in your closet, on a clothes line in your laundry room, or wherever you can find some space. This is especially important for dress shirts and T-shirts. A dryer will not only shrink these but will seriously shorten their life.

So how do you iron clothes? Well, you'll first need a few basic tools.

One iron—you can use a steam iron, but the method I describe below does not use the steam option. Standard irons usually range from twelve hundred to eighteen hundred watts, with some higher-end models going up from there. All this really has to do with is how fast the iron heats up, not how hot it actually gets. A standard iron will run you about thirty bucks and should last for years.

One standard-size ironing board—those dorm-sized travel boards are just plain silly and don't work. Don't use them. You'll need something sturdy with a top that you're comfortable ironing on.

You will also need a spray bottle and some clothes to iron.

So first, spray your shirt down with water from the spray bottle—if you are ironing your shirt straight from the washer, you can skip this step. That is actually an advantage of ironing right from the washer.

Plug in the iron and set the temperature gauge to the type of cloth you are ironing. If you're not sure, check the label. And then place the damp shirt on the ironing board. Spread the collar out on the ironing board—you'll be ironing under the collar first. Iron and turn the collar over and repeat.

Place the damp shirt on the ironing board so the back of the shirt is flat and iron it. Now, if at any time, if the shirt begins to dry out, spray the cloth down again, just so it's damp.

Flatten the sleeves against the board and iron the sleeves. Flatten one cuff on the ironing board and iron it, then take that sleeve by the seam and lay the whole sleeve flat on the ironing board. If you can see the crease on the top of the sleeve from previous ironing, try to match it again so that you have a single crease line on the sleeve. Repeat with the other sleeve.

Iron the front of the shirt. With the collar to your left, place the left side of the shirt on your ironing board. Iron around the collar and then down, smoothing it with your hand, if needed. Keep rotating, smoothing, and ironing until you come to the right front of the shirt. Iron the top section first, then the rest of it.

Now ironing pants is pretty easy and only has two real steps:

First, hook the pants over the tip of the board so the upper thigh part of the pants is flat. Iron that part. Repeat on the other end. Then, find the crease of the pant and fold along the crease. Iron the front crease and the back. Repeat on the other leg.

And that's it.

Ironing is a little thing that adds such a big impact to your appearance. You may not ever notice a shirt that is perfectly ironed, but see a wrinkled one and your eyes won't be able to leave it.

Homesteading

There is a great quote by Robert Heinlein that goes, "Every generation thinks it invented sex."

Yup. We do. And not just sex; every generation thinks it was the first to discover . . . everything.

We arrive in the world and we begin to see and experience. And when we see and experience, we assume that what we see and experience has not been seen or experienced before. How could it be? We just found out about this marvelous thing ourselves, and because we're the center of it all, how could anything of any importance have occurred before we got here, or before it involved us?

It can't. And because it's all new to us, it must all be new.

Makes sense. Except for the fact that it's all been done before. And just because we are now experiencing something for the first time doesn't make it new.

The Bible says, "What has been will be again, what has been done will be done again; there is nothing new under the sun" (Ecclesiastes 1:9).

And there isn't.

With the exception of every generation's new technological gizmos that keep coming out, and will always be coming out, everything important has already been done before.

And this isn't a bad thing.

What is a bad thing is when we think we should get credit for discovering something just because we've renamed it or repackaged it. There aren't new discoveries; there are only new movements.

Eating only food that will go to waste if we don't eat it doesn't get to be called "freeganism." It's what people have been doing for centuries and still do every day around the world.

Making use of the materials you have doesn't get to be called "repurposing" or even "recycling;" it's just plain good sense and what's been done since—forever.

Now, there's another new twist on an old idea that has popped up in the past few years that isn't new at all, but is still pretty intriguing. It's the old concept of homesteading.

The pure definition of homesteading dates back to the 1862 and the U.S. Homestead Act. It is the ability to establish a home in unsettled land and get everything you need from that land. You get your food from your garden, your fruit trees, and your livestock. You get what currency you need from the sale of said items, by bartering, or through other means. You take care of the land and the land takes care of you.

The term *homesteading* is pretty commonly known and we all have a general idea of what that means. You go someplace where few people live and you live there and farm.

Sort of.

The true definition of the term *homesteading* has to do with subsistence farming or living a self-sufficient lifestyle—more modern terms for old ideas. But what makes this modern trend an interesting one is that there is now land out there that developers have no interest in—in every state, probably within two to three hours from where you are right now—that is cheap.

And I mean dirt cheap. In fact, for less than the cost of a big-screen TV, you can get a few acres of land—and some plots for even less than that.

Now, these are homesteading lots—undeveloped lots. Most don't have power or water or much of anything except the land itself. But they are cheap and they are plentiful.

In recent years, homesteading has been placed in an ultra-liberal, almost radical box through the use of phrases such as *self-sufficiency* and *living off the grid*. But the act of homesteading simply means taking responsibility for yourself through your land.

Now, the reason I'm bringing all of this up is not to promote the idea of homesteading. I think it's a great concept for the right people, but I also think it can be used as an excuse to pull away from society and the neighbors who need you.

What I do want to promote—and I think that this *does* apply to everyone—is the fact that there is cheap land out there. It may be on a hill, covered in trees, and probably will never see a power connection or a water line, but it's affordable. And the thing about land is that they are not making any more of it.

There is something in our core that makes us want to own land—and this goes back further than generations; it's why our ancestors came here in the first place. It's that land, that entity that they aren't making any more of, that has always driven people.

Today, for a few thousand bucks, you can own a few acres of land. And if you only throw up a tent there a few times a year, if you only go to it to show your friends, if you only build a shack or a cabin or an A-frame on it, it's still your land. And if you pay the few hundred dollars a year in taxes, it will be yours forever.

That flat screen will be gone. That dream vacation will be a distant memory. But your land will always be there.

Your land. A place you can visit or a place you can live. A place you can hand down or a place you can sell.

Because once you check out of that hotel room or that cruise ship docks, your lease is up and that place is no longer yours.

Skill #220:

How to Choose a Watch

Before the 1920s, many men swore that they would sooner wear a dress than be seen wearing a watch. Or, more specifically, a wristwatch.

Now, the standard watch—what was known as the pocket watch—was an acceptable male accoutrement for hundreds of years. In fact, up through the nineteenth century, most men owned a pocket watch, and it was very common for a father's watch to be handed down to his son and keep moving down through the family across generations—I even have my great-grandfather's pocket watch.

A wristwatch, however, was considered a lady's watch. It was a decorative piece of jewelry that women wore on their wrists and was actually called a "wristlet." It wasn't until World War I, when soldiers strapped their pocket watches to their wrists to synchronize attacks, that the wristwatch began to slowly move into vogue among men.

Today, even with clocks on our phones, laptops, and iPads, a watch is still a classic male adornment. And choosing the right watch can be a difficult decision. In fact, many men simply choose to purchase a disposable watch—something cheap that they can simply replace when it dies, rather that choosing a watch they can wear for years.

So how do you choose a watch? Well there are a few things to consider.

Shape and Material
With the popular watches, you'll see rectangular, square, and other funky crystal shapes. But the reality is that a crystal has a chance to break or leak at the corners. No corners and your chance of allowing water in or a seal to crack are reduced. So, the classic round face is the best way to go.

Budget
The diamond industry set the standard that a man should spend two months' salary on the engagement ring he chooses. This is nuts. And it is only based on what the jewelry folks want you to spend.

The watch industry has a standard that is a little more realistic. It states that a man should spend on a watch ten times what he spends on lunch for a week. So, if you brown-bag it, then a three-hundred-dollar watch is about right. If you go to the drive-thru every day, then a five-hundred-dollar watch is more your speed. If you eat at a Friday's or Olive Garden, then you should buy a seven-hundred-dollar watch, and if you eat at a place with tablecloths and a wine list, you should spend a thousand bucks for your watch.

Do your research and find the watch you like, and then look for a used watch in that type. Look on eBay, Craigslist, at pawn shops, or in thrift stores.

Style
Your watch signifies who you are. It will convey your style, your mind-set, and your image. Your watch doesn't have to cost more than your car, but it does need to be a high-quality timepiece. Remember, a watch is an investment. It tells people where you are and where you intend to go. Buying

a cheap watch says that the watch is disposable. But buying a watch that is outside of your budget may say that you are irresponsible.

Remember: Choose quality and take your time.

It's not uncommon for someone to have a watch he or she keeps for a few decades. And it's not uncommon for people to have a few watches—that daily watch, that dress-up watch, and maybe one you wear when chopping wood or wrestling bears.

With me, I have only one watch: my Swiss Army watch that has been through five bands and a dozen batteries but still works like a charm. It's been banged around, beat up, and smashed against things. But it never complains.

Thieves

There was an article posted a while back about a church that had the sound equipment for its big sunrise Easter service stolen. The service takes place outside and is attended by more than a thousand people, and without that equipment, there would be no way for the large crowd to hear the music or the pastor. The church would have to cancel the service if it didn't have the sound equipment. But what was interesting about the story was that when the church discovered the theft, discussed what happened, and—they prayed for the thieves. They forgave them. They went into their budget and rented sound equipment and the service went on as scheduled.

Now, what's even more fascinating about this story is when you look at it from a different angle—at the people who took the equipment—you can tell a few things about them. See, most thieves did not set out to be thieves. Absolutely not. They didn't tell their guidance counselors that's what they wanted to do. They didn't set thief goals. They didn't dream about being the greatest thieves ever and they didn't brag at high school reunions of how one day they would steal sound equipment from churches. It just happened. Stealing became the default. The fallback. And it usually happens for one simple reason.

They got desperate.

There are few people that steal for the pure pleasure of it. There may be a few—a celebrity shoplifter, an Ivy League hacker—but they are the exception. The idea of the millionaire cat burglar taking jewels for the thrill of the challenge is fiction. Because nobody has a great day stealing. No thief takes pride in their work. No thief feels good about what they do. They get desperate. Then they get stupid. In fact, every stupid thing we do, have done, and will ever do, is because we got desperate. Which means we got stupid. And then we say those words. *I have no choice.* We get in a corner and our options seem limited.

Which is a lie. No matter what—every time—we always have options. We always have choices.

Why do millions of people fall for Internet and email scams every year? That's easy. Because they are so desperate that they need those cons to be true—wealthy people don't fall for these things; desperate people do. They are in dire need for money, their options seem limited, and they think: *If this were true, it would fix everything.* They switch off their intelligence because they need it to be true: *This has to work because there is no other choice.*

And when you go even further, when you boil that desperation down, what do you have? What is at the core of desperation?

Fear.

Desperation is the fear that the alternative, the next step, is so terrible that we have to do *this horrible thing* to make sure that *other horrible thing* doesn't happen.

Stealing is less scary than going without that next fix or that next drink. Stealing is less risky than waking up and having to face the world clear-headed. Taking this stuff is far less scary than having to face all the bad decisions we've made and take a different route. So, we cross that line. We pop open that church's storage trailer and, fueled by desperation, we grab that sound equipment. And what happens then?

Nothing. Nothing happens. We get that sound equipment and we get it to a pawn shop and we get the money. And when we wake up the next morning, there aren't people pounding on our door. We don't hear sirens wailing toward us. The world doesn't end. Nothing happened.

Not to us, anyway. But something always happens.

Several years ago, my wife's ninety-year-old grandmother had her house robbed while she was out. The thieves got away with two old televisions and some costume jewelry. Total take: around four hundred dollars.

When Beulah—yes, that's her real name—came home, she was shocked. She called the police and she called her family. A new lock was put on the house and a new television was purchased. But the story didn't end there.

Beulah couldn't sleep after that. She was so worried about the thieves coming back that she became completely preoccupied with this idea. She stopped sleeping and eating altogether. She would call family all hours of the night and tell them that someone was upstairs. And one night a neighbor found Beulah in her driveway in just a nightgown, running from the house because she was convinced the thieves had come back for her.

Beulah went into a nursing home shortly after that because she couldn't focus on anything other than the thieves. And when she died a few years later, she was still obsessed with that break-in.

Now, did those thieves kill Beulah?

No. Probably not. But they did take the joy and security out of the few years she had left. No doubt about that. And they did it for four hundred dollars.

But the good thing for the thieves is that they will never know that—that's the only career advantage in being a thief.

You steal, you run, and you never have to look your victims in the eye. The consequences are kept far, far away from you.

When we get desperate, we get stupid. We change. And we change the world around us. Every time.

Two thousand years ago, two other thieves faced their own last hours on Earth. They thought about their lives and they considered all that they had done.

One became humble—he was the rare one.

And the other one remained desperate.

Skill #78:

Brewing a Real Cup of Coffee

Electric coffeemakers are wonderful things. We take cold water and ground coffee and put them in a machine. We push a button and even before we've read through our morning emails, there is a fresh pot of coffee waiting for us. Ding! Depending on the brand of coffeemaker, the overall brew time is between four and seven minutes. Not bad.

The modern coffeemaker can trace its roots back to 1972, when Mr. Coffee came out with the first commercially successful automatic drip coffeemaker. Before that, every kitchen in America had either an electric coffee percolator or a coffeepot that was placed on the stove.

The electric coffee percolator is that device you've seen in every episode of *The Brady Bunch* and *Leave It to Beaver*. It's a metal pot that you fill with water. Inside, a long stem fits in the bottom of the pot and a basket attaches to the top, where you place the ground coffee. As the temperature rises, the water in the bottom of the chamber boils and travels up the stem to the basket. The hot water is distributed over the dry coffee and leaches back into the pot. Depending on the brand of percolator you use, a full pot of coffee in an electric percolator should take anywhere from seven to eleven minutes to make.

The newest coffee innovation is the K-cup-style coffee machine. This was created by Keurig—the "K" in the term *K-cup*—which, in 1998, introduced a single-cup coffeemaker designed for office use. In this machine, a K-cup—a sealed plastic cup of coffee, hot chocolate, tea, or other beverage—is placed in the machine, water is added, you push the button, and you have one cup of the exact type of coffee you want. Then your cubicle mate can get another cup of a different-flavored coffee. The machine was a success, and the company branched out into home-style units. Now, everyone from Folgers to Dunkin' Donuts offers coffee in a K-cup option. The time to brew one cup on a Keurig coffeemaker is just a couple of minutes.

The average American consumes 3.1 cups of coffee a day (9 ounces), which may not seem like much, but in fact, it is second only to milk and beats soda and energy drinks by a wide margin. And the coffee market is such that you can now get a mocha latte at McDonald's or have a dozen different types of coffee to choose from at the station where you pump your gas. But real coffee—simple and classic coffee—is easy to make, takes about the same time as the other methods, and costs pennies compared to that twelve-dollar venti triple mocha.

The rules here are simple. Get yourself a classic coffeepot—not a teapot, but an old-fashioned coffeepot that sits on the stove. The electric kind won't work here because you need to get the water to a rolling boil. Also, you want a standard coffeepot that is a cylinder, not one that is tapered and larger on the bottom—you'll see why in a minute. Here's what you do:

1. Take out the coffee stem and basket and set aside—you'll need these later.

2. Fill your coffeepot with water and add a pinch of salt—this takes some of the bitterness out of the coffee.

3. Bring the water to a rolling boil.

4. Now, remove the pot from the heat and wait thirty seconds—this is important because if you add the coffee right after the water has been boiling, it will flash up and the grounds will cling to the inside of the pot. You'll not only have grounds in your coffee when you pour, but you'll also waste coffee.

5. Add the coffee directly into the water, stirring if needed. This is to allow the coffee to brew in the water and not get burned by the constant boiling if you use the coffeepot as it was intended, which is to fill the basket with coffee, boil it, and let it brew for ten minutes. This new method may seem strange because the coffee is now off the heat, but it works.

6. Cover the pot and let it sit for six minutes—ten minutes will create a dark, richer coffee that many people like, but six minutes is where I like it myself.

7. Take the basket and drop it into the pot, then take the stem with the large part down and drop it into the pot. You would think the stem could fit the other way but it is slightly smaller to allow the basket to sit on the stem.

8. Slowly press the basket down, pressing the coffee and keeping the grounds on the bottom.

9. Hold the stem down and pour.

Now, when you try this for the first time, the coffee may taste weaker than what you are accustomed to. And that could be because coffee is very easy to burn, and often, that rich taste we've gotten used to at the gas station or the diner is actually burnt coffee! It could also be because bolder-flavored coffees are often perceived as having more caffeine, and therefore, we want our coffee to be as dark and bold as possible—when in actuality, the lighter roast coffees have the most caffeine.

Making coffee like this won't change your life drastically, and you may only use this method a few times. But knowing about it allows you to add one more skill to your growing list. And knowledge is always a fun thing to carry around.

The Fifty-Year-Old You

Medifast, a nutrition and weight-loss company, came up with an advertising campaign a few years ago that was not only very creative, but extremely powerful. The company filmed a woman at the beginning of her fitness journey, having a conversation with someone in a chair next to her—only there was no one in that chair. She was speaking to the chair as if the new version of herself were sitting there, twelve weeks into the program.

At the end of the twelve weeks, the same woman came back and sat in the new chair and responded to the now-empty chair on her left, as if she were having a conversation with herself from twelve weeks earlier. Through some video magic, these two films were edited into a seamless conversation.

In the ads, we see the old version of the person—beaten, discouraged, and afraid—being encouraged by the new version, who is strong, fit, and confident. Of course, the new individual is not afraid of anything, because the new one knows what will happen. The new you holds all the secrets.

Today, I have done the same thing for you—the you of today (for those of you who are under the age of fifty). I've gone into the future and found you at fifty years old. We have spoken and I have brought that person here to talk to you and tell you a few things. This version of you wants to talk to his/her twenty-year-old, thirty-year-old, even forty-year-old self, not only to let you know what to expect but to give you a few insights and cheats for the next few decades.

Here are the five things that the fifty-year-old you wants you to know.

You Look Good.

Yes, there will come a point—ten, twenty, or thirty years from now—when you will look at a picture of yourself at this current point in time—it could even be a picture that is being taken at this very moment—and the new you is going to smile and think, "Wow, I wasn't bad-looking back then."

Today is the best you will look. Now, this might sound like bad news, but it's not. It does not mean that your appearance will degrade from now on. It just means that you won't appreciate your appearance until it does.

And that's the clincher. There will never, ever be a time when the exact amount you appreciate how you look meets the exact way you look. It just doesn't happen. Because by the time you do appreciate it, time has moved on and you're looking back at a photograph and wishing you still looked like that now.

Here is the paradox: If the thirty-year-old you were looking at a photograph of the twenty-year-old you, he would wish he looked like that now. And if you took a picture of that you looking at that picture, the forty-year-old you would look at the thirty-year-old you and wish the same thing.

Which means that someday you will want to look like exactly the way you do right now. Learn to appreciate it while you have the chance.

Most of the Time, You're Kind of a Jerk.

Although your physical appearance is just fine the way it is, your view of life kind of sucks. In your twenties, thirties, and even forties, your skin is far too thin and your self-involvement levels are way too high—so much so that if you and the fifty-year-old version of you were talking at a party, the older version would politely excuse him- or herself and find someone more interesting to talk to.

Insecurity runs deep, and when you mix that with our need for acceptance, the end result is a highly internalized, afraid, and somewhat shallow individual.

What's the evidence? The fifty-year-old version of yourself rarely takes a selfie. The twenty-, thirty-, and forty-year-old versions may have dozens of them scattered across various social networks, but not so many later on. Also, the fifty-year-old you uses the word *I* far less than the current you does, but uses the words *we* and *us* a lot more.

Now, mix this self-involvement along with another trait that the younger version of you has: the need to be right. The younger version of you not only needs to be right, but also needs to prove to other people that he or she is right—no matter what.

Although you may build houses for the poor and read to the blind in your free time, your twenty-, thirty-, and even forty-year-old attitude needs a little tweaking. Eventually, your confidence will increase and you'll settle into a solid view of the world, but until then, relax, take the focus off yourself, and think.

Money Is Better Than Stuff.
This may seem like a somewhat cold view of life, but it's actually the opposite. The fifty-year-old you knows that money—meaning the actual currency that you've earned and built up—is far better than the things you can buy with that currency.

Yes, there will be a day when you are looking at that photo album and you'll miss that car you had when you were twenty or that motorcycle you rode to Maine on. But in reality, you're not missing the tangible car; you're missing the places you went in it, you're missing the friends who rode with you to Maine.

As cold and nonpoetic as it sounds, the fifty-year-old you knows that there is confidence to be had in working hard and having a nest egg—actual currency saved—rather than a box full of toys. Also, the fifty-year-old you knows the feeling of having cash if someone needs your help or if there is a charity you believe in, or even if you want to start one of your own.

That same internalized pride we had in our twenties spreads out once we hit fifty. We become less proud of us and prouder of those who contributed to who we are.

Being Fifty Is Something to Look Forward to, Not Fear.
The fifty-year-old version of you is happy, excited, hardworking, and confident. By the time you hit fifty, you are hitting your stride and looking forward to each day and each new challenge. The fifty-year-old you has a view of life that is clear and accurate; he or she knows what's important and what's not. The fifty-year-old you laughs more and worries less.

And the fifty-year-old you can't wait to meet you.

How to Pack a Lunch

In the early 1800s, almost seventy percent of all American families lived on farms. Most of these were subsistence farms—a few cows, pigs, chickens, on some land where corn, wheat, and potatoes were planted. These farms were their families' main source of food and clothing. The farmer would rise early and feed his livestock, repair fences, fix machinery, gather eggs, and in the middle of the day, when he would need some food and a short break, he would walk back to his house to visit with his wife and children and eat a small meal. For hundreds of years, the term *lunch* simply meant that: to take a break from your work and go home to eat.

As the effects of the Industrial Revolution spread, factories and mills needed more and more workers. Now, the small farmer had the opportunity not only to care for his land but to travel to town for day work in order to bring some additional income into the household. And because it would not be practical for the farmer to return home for lunch—and because he would need to leave early in the morning and not return until late that night—he would have to take food with him.

So, the farmer would put hard-boiled eggs, biscuits, vegetables, and meat into a container—often a small basket with a handle—and head out in the morning. He would meet up with other men who were carrying similar baskets as well as those with meals wrapped in handkerchiefs or placed in metal tins. Workers in more extreme environments—such as coal mines and steel mills—needed something to transport their lunch in that would protect it, so they often used small covered milk pails.

By the 1850s, manufacturers saw a growing consumer need for a container to carry lunches in, so they began to mass-produce fitted metal buckets and boxes specifically designed for this. They were called "lunch pails" even though the trend was leaning more toward the box style. They sold well and the need continued.

In 1904, the thermos was introduced as an option to the commercial lunch pail. Now a worker could have a cold lunch with a hot drink. And when schools began to regionalize—with the one-room school transforming into larger, multigrade schools—children were now unable to come home for lunch. Like their working fathers, they also needed to take their lunches with them, and many wanted to mimic their fathers, seeking out metal pails or buckets to carry their food in.

In 1935, the first children's lunchbox with a licensed character was produced: The image of Mickey Mouse was lithographed over an oval tin with a handle. And in 1950, the first TV character made the cut, Hopalong Cassidy, on a lunchbox that cost two dollars and sold half a million units in the first year alone.

For decades, there seemed to be two basic types of lunchbox: the metal work style for adults and the metal-boxed character style for kids—with a picture of their favorite TV show, band, or sports figure on the side.

But when a child moved from elementary school to high school, the lunchbox was often abandoned. In that socially sensitive environment, there was a need for young people to distance themselves from childish things and the brown paper bag became a safer choice for a lunch container. Plus, you could now purchase a hot lunch from the school cafeteria.

Today, the average American purchases lunch rather than bringing it and spends an average of ten dollars on each lunch trip, with the majority of those meals bought at fast-food restaurants. We eat in our car. We eat on the run. And we eat whatever is quickly made and cheaply provided. Whether it's because of our memories of soggy bologna sandwiches or the need to continue to distance ourselves from childish things, few of us bring a lunch to work. If we do, it's a quickly prepared sandwich that we eat at our desk.

But the bagged lunch as an entity, as a creative endeavor, is an amazing thing. It is healthier, far less expensive (we spend around two thousand dollars a year on fast-food lunches), and gives us control over our day. It's a very neat thing.

The first step is to get yourself a lunchbox—and I mean one that fits your needs as well as your lifestyle. A brown paper bag is only temporary; choosing a container to bring your lunch in shows a commitment to seeing it through.

Here are some quick options for lunch ideas.

Leftovers
This is an easy and simple. Simply take some of that lasagna from last night or some of that leftover casserole and bring it to work in a Tupperware container. Provided you have access to a refrigerator and a microwave, this works well.

Soup
There is nothing like a cup of hot soup with a biscuit or some bread in the middle of the day. And the great thing

here is that you can be working in the middle of the woods and still bring hot soup in a thermos, provided you made it up beforehand.

Wraps

Only because sandwiches are so overplayed—and because most store-bought bread is pretty tasteless and gets soggy incredibly fast—wraps are a good alternative. You can make a wrap using cold cuts and cheese. They are smaller than a sandwich, can be made quicker, and are easier to eat on the run.

Mason Jars

This idea may be a little played out, but I still think it's pretty cool.

What you do is take a mason jar, and in the bottom, you put in your wet ingredients: for example, your salad dressing. Then you add in the solid vegetables—anything that won't get soggy if they touch the dressing—cut-up tomatoes, cucumbers, red onion, celery, peppers, lettuce, and so on. Then you add your softer items: pasta, beans, avocado. On top of that put your protein: chicken, turkey, beans. And then on the very top goes your cheese and any nuts.

The downside to this is that you need to fill the jar so the food items don't shift. Which means you need to add it to a separate bowl before eating, which takes away from it being a self-contained meal. But it does give you the advantage of being able to make up many jars ahead of time—some people make a week's worth in advance. The salad remains in the jar until you need it, then you pour it into a bowl where all the ingredients mix. Genius.

So, get creative, get a lunch box, and get to work.

Grab a bag, a bucket, or a mason jar and pack yourself a lunch. McDonald's will survive without you and the thousands of dollars you save each year can go toward a fun trip—like going to the Lunch Box Museum in Columbus, Georgia.

What Your Health Club Won't Tell You

Let's say you open a bakery.

You are now the proud owner and operator of Tralfaz Bakery.

Congratulations.

Which means that you went out, found a location, bought equipment, hired some people, opened your doors, and you are now in the baked goods business.

Now, the first question is: How do you make your money? How does Tralfaz Bakery operate?

Well, it's pretty straightforward. You produce income by selling baked goods to the public. And you do this by purchasing raw materials—flour, sugar, eggs—and then using those raw materials to make sellable goods—breads, cookies, and cakes. You mark up these goods accordingly, and when you sell them, you can not only cover your overhead and invest back into the business, but also pay for more raw materials to make more sellable goods.

Boom.

The business model for your bakery is clear and linear. The more goods you sell, the more money you make. And as long as this process is not interrupted, as long as your costs and your customer base don't change, the bakery will continue on successfully.

Now, let's say you get bored with Tralfaz Bakery. You sell it and buy Tralfaz Motors, a car dealership. Which means that you make a profit by selling new cars. But in order to sell those new cars, you take in customers' old cars in trade and resell them. You also make a profit on the extras you sell to the customer: extended warrantees, service plans, and rust treatments. And you also make a profit on servicing and repairing the cars that you sell and on the markup of the parts you stock to repair those cars.

Your business model is still clear—even though it has multiple income streams—and is still linear. You make money by selling cars, car repair, and maintenance services.

Okay, last one. You wake up one morning and sell Tralfaz Motors and decide to open up—ta-da—Tralfaz Fitness, a full-service health club.

So, how do you make your money?

Well, if you own a health club, that means that you went out and leased or bought a building. You stocked it with exercise equipment for both cardio and strength training. You allocated safe areas for fitness classes, as well as shower and locker space for customers. You hired fitness professionals and you priced memberships to cover your costs and build in profit. Then you determined how many guests you can support at that facility, as well as how many guests you need to come in just to cover your costs.

As long as the customers keep coming in, as long as the number of members remains between the base number you need to cover costs and the maximum number you can service from that facility, you'll continue to operate successfully.

And that is what we call . . . a lie.

That is not how health clubs operate.

At all.

Not even a little bit.

Health clubs operate by selling long-term memberships to people and then—here comes the good part—incentivizing them to *never come in*.

Ever.

A health club makes its money selling annuities—long-term financial commitments that produce an ongoing income stream at a one-hundred-percent profit margin. Health clubs sell air.

"What?" you might say. "That's ridiculous."

But no. It's not. Don't believe me? Let's look at a few things.

An average corporate gym has about ten thousand paid members. But only two thousand of those members actually use the facility for more than a few months. One-fifth of the people who purchase these memberships—never go at all.

One of the biggest gym chains in the country has facilities that can support around three hundred members per site. Yet each site signs up in excess of six thousand members.

"Okay," you might argue, "but that's not the gym's fault. If people aren't disciplined enough to keep coming, that's their own problem."

But here is an interesting question. How many employees at the gym are incentivized by sales? How do they make money? By the number of pounds members lose? By members reaching their fitness goals? By how happy the customer base is?

Nope. They make money by selling new memberships.

In fact, almost all health club employees have a sales quota that they need to meet each month. The high employee turnaround is largely because individuals can't meet these sales goals.

Here's a fun experiment. Track the response you get when you walk into the gym and ask for information on joining. Then track the response when you walk in a week later and ask for a towel.

The employees are not incentivized to give you towels. Travis, your buddy who signed you up for that great three-year deal, doesn't even remember your name now. In fact, the employees are financially motivated to make sure you stop coming to the gym.

Look at what happens at a gym between the time you sign up and the time you stop going. Let's say you haven't been there in a month. Two months. Four. What happens?

Well, that's easy. Nothing happens. Nothing at all.

No calls. No email reminders. No encouragement to come back. Because the gym doesn't want you to come back. If you do, you are wearing down the equipment, using the water and towels, and cutting into the profit margin. But if you stay away—that's pure profit.

And that's what gyms really are: financial institutions. They sell long-term financial agreements to customers, then they go the bank and show the cash flow. In fact, gyms then take all this financial billing and sell it to another company. *They aren't even the one collecting your money.* By the time you are out the door after signing up, your payment has been transferred to the finance company and the gym hopes you never come back.

These annuities are the entire structure of the health club's business model. Gyms have a solid cash flow based on the complicated contracts with members, and there is no limit to the number of new members they can sign up. The only limitation is the demographic limits of the region where the gym is located. If it could, a health club that can support only three hundred members would gladly sign up ten thousand or more.

Here is a quick test. Walk into your gym after you've signed up and gauge the response you get from the staff.

Then turn around and walk into your bank and gauge the response you get from the staff. The bank will be all over you: "Good morning, how are we doing today? Is there anything else I can do for you? Thanks for banking with us."

Why are they so friendly? Because they know you can leave your bank. But leaving your gym is a little more complicated. Not only are there serious fees and penalties for canceling, but the structure itself is designed to keep you from ever stopping your membership.

Recently, I decided that I didn't want to spend twenty dollars a month—along with the high yearly fee—for the right to carry a key tag with the gym name on it around with me. So, after years of membership, I called to cancel.

I was told that I could not cancel over the phone. I had to come in.

So I went in. Then I was told that I had to cancel with a manager and had to come in when one was on duty.

So, I went back when a manager was on duty. But the manager was tied up. I made an appointment to meet with the manager the following week.

When I got there a week later, the manager was tied up again and I waited. But the manager never came out.

After about four months of this, I called and said that I could not catch a manager and needed to cancel my membership *immediately*. I was told that if I mailed in a certified letter stating that I wanted to cancel, that would take care of everything.

So, I wrote a letter and sent it in certified. A few weeks later, the receipt came back to me signed.

There. Done.

Then I noticed the next month that I was not only billed again for the month, but the yearly fee had been billed as well.

I made a copy of the certified letter and drove down to the gym to meet with a manager (who, of course, wasn't there). I left the copy of the letter with a message to call my cell phone ASAP.

Three days later, after I did not hear back, I called and asked for a manager. She was tied up. After telling the person on the phone that I would stay on hold *forever*, the manager suddenly became free.

She looked up my account, saw that the certified letter had come in, saw that it was processed and that it was filed. And—congratulations. Done. I had now successfully *given my one-month notice.*

What?

"Yes, sir," she explained. "When you signed up, you agreed to give us a month's written notice if you ever wanted to cancel. So, after being billed next month, your membership will end."

What does all this mean? That gyms are evil?

No. But it does mean they can be unethical, that their business model is deceptive and their practices are designed to get us to pay for something we don't use.

It's an illusion.

So, what's the answer?

Well, just because you go to a health club doesn't mean you're healthy. And just because you don't go to a health club doesn't mean you're not.

You are in control of your health.

And your money.

You need to determine what you are going to do—and no prepackaged health club membership can do that for you. You decide.

Maybe it's walking on Sunday morning, biking to work, or learning tai chi. The danger is that we allow the gym membership to give us false comfort. Just because we can go anytime we want, twenty-four hours a day, in twenty-three separate locations, doesn't mean we will.

Skill #419:

How to Cook Pizza on the Grill

My backyard grill is one of my all-time favorite personal possessions. In fact, if I could keep only three items that would be mine and mine alone, they would be:

:: My bike;

:: My Swiss Army watch—yeah, I have a Swiss Army knife, too, but my watch is great; and

:: My grill.

As long as my family was safe and they had all they needed, I would be extremely content with just owning these three things for myself.

I have a Weber Spirit. It's a great grill. With the three burners, I can do pretty much anything, and one of my favorite things to do on the grill is pizza. It's fun, unique, and with the high heat of the grill, you can get that brick-oven crunch—also, we are ex–New Yorkers who now live in Delaware, and there is no decent pizza here.

Now, the method I use for pizza is based on trial and error from a three-burner grill like my Weber Spirit. I have tried other grilled pizza techniques and this one works really well, but you'll need to experiment with your particular grill.

Cooking a pizza on a grill is pretty easy. A very simple way to do it is to purchase a one-pound bag of commercial pizza dough—or make your own dough. Pizza Bud is the brand I buy. It costs only eighty-eight cents and I can get two pizzas out of one bag of dough.

Cut a sixteen-ounce dough ball in half.

With a rolling pin, roll out the dough. Yes, the pizza-tossing thing is very cool, but you need to be good at that and I am not. So, a rolling pin is a great way to get an even crust. Also, roll your dough out longways instead of as a traditional round pie. This allows you to get up to four pizzas on your grill and reduces the chance of burning. And don't worry about making the shape perfect. The more imperfect it is, the more it takes on that "brick-oven-made look."

Over low heat—again, this is based on a three-burner grill—place the dough directly on the grill.

Wait three minutes or so and flip the dough. Wait another three minutes and pull the dough from the grill. This will be your pizza crust.

Take the dough off the grill and move to a cutting board to prep it. With the most cooked end facing up, cover lightly with some olive oil. Now, build your pizza—cheese, sauce, pepperoni, spices, whatever you want—and place back it directly on the grill. If you are sliding it on, the toppings will stay on place, and as the pizza cooks, they will melt into the cheese.

Close the grill and allow the pizza to cook. Check every few minutes and look at the bottom of the pizza—this will tell you how the pizza is cooking. Keep in mind that there is a thin line between getting that perfect brick-oven crunch and burning the bottom of the pizza. If you're not sure, pull the pizza early.

Let the pizza cool for five minutes and cut it.

One of the greatest things about cooking a pizza on the grill is that it's very simple, but seems so exotic. Mention to someone that you had pizza on the grill last night and the common response is: How do you do that?

Well—now you know.

The Understanding of Plenty

Just a few years ago, when my mom still lived at home, I used to visit her as often as I could at the house I grew up in, in the Catskills of New York.

Now, people were always—and I mean always—impressed at my mother's age back then; she was ninety-two. And they were impressed even before you added in all the *ands*: She was ninety-two years old *and* still lived at home. She was ninety-two years old *and* still drove her own car. She still took care of her own bills, made her own meals, bought her own groceries, made muffins every Sunday for church, and had the most active social life of any of us. If you wanted my mother to do something with you, you had to choose a Tuesday or a Thursday, her most flexible days.

At ninety-two, my mother remembered every family member's birthday—including every niece, grandchild, and great-grandchild, but she could also go back to her grandparents and their extended families. Every summer, we all traveled for up to nine hours to descend on her Walton, New York, home for the weekend to have a family reunion.

Now, before you think my mother is some kind of perfect human, it's important to know that she . . . well, she sees the world a little bit differently. And this has nothing to do with her age; this is just her.

Here's an example.

When I was in my twenties, a young guy on his own, I went to my parents' home for the weekend. And like many young guys, I brought a bag of laundry with me to do while I was there. So, I did the laundry, the weekend passed, and on Sunday night, I said good-bye to my parents and drove the sixty miles back to my apartment in Binghamton, New York.

When Monday morning came, my mother got up and noticed that I had left some underwear in the dryer.

Oh no, my mother thought. *My child is out there in the world without all of his clean underwear.*

So, Velma De Morier put the underwear in a clear—and this is a very important part of the story—a *clear* plastic bag and hightailed it the sixty miles to deliver the much-needed underwear to her son.

I had a small apartment at the time. My mother knew exactly where this apartment was and it provided several ideal places where you could discreetly drop off underwear if needed—a fact I insisted on before signing the lease. But this situation was much more urgent than that, so my mother headed straight to where I worked. And because I worked for a large corporation, she drove around the buildings, trying to find the main entrance. When she couldn't, she saw some people outside one of the buildings on a smoke break.

"Do you know my son?" my mother asked.

Because there were more than a thousand employees and I hadn't been there all that long, the man she asked didn't know me. So, my mother gave the man the clear bag of underwear and instructed him to give it to me. The poor guy walked the clear bag of underwear to the main building's secretary. Who walked it to the second building's secretary. Who gave it to the sales secretary. Who called and got the purchasing secretary to pick it up. Who was given the bag and was nice enough to drop it off on my cubicle chair.

In twenty minutes, my underwear saw more of those buildings than I did for the two years I worked there.

Now, the fascinating aspect of this story is that when you tell it to my mother, she looks at you with a "Yeah? What's your point?" expression. From her perspective, there is absolutely nothing wrong with what she did. There was a job to do and she did it. Over.

I have dozens of stories like this—stories where she had a pond dug out for us and then a few hours later realized that ponds were dangerous and had it filled back in. Stories where I heard knocking on my apartment door and opened it to find four firemen standing there because my phone had tipped off the hook and my mother thought the apartment had filled with gas. There are even a few stories about how my mother nearly drowned me trying to teach me to swim— she can't swim a stroke but she still figured she knew enough to teach the basic skills.

When it comes to my mother, we're dealing with someone who sees the world from a unique perspective.

Which is one of her biggest strengths.

Every Thanksgiving, my mother and my mother-in-law come down to stay with us for a few days. During this time, I take both of them to an Amish general store nearby that has everything from craft items to discount canned goods. Both women love it and I have a great time going through every aisle with my mom as she picks out her canned goods— canned peaches, three for a dollar; peas and carrots, fifty cents a can. She is an excited person.

Now, when I take my mother home, she places her canned goods and dry goods in her already-full pantry. Which brings me to the point.

My mother has a kitchen full of canned fruits and vegetables, canned soups, muffin mixes, frozen meat, and coffee. That's pretty much all she wants and all she needs.

And every day—if she's not out to dinner with someone—she walks out to her kitchen and opens a can of soup or warms up some stewed tomatoes. That's her dinner and that's all she wants.

She *never*—and I mean *never*—walks into her kitchen and says, "There's nothing to eat here." She *never*—and I mean *never*—looks at the canned goods and says, "Ugh, I feel like pizza instead." And she *never*—and I mean *never*—feels like she is skimping or going without.

The strange part is that my mother is a very particular person. She likes her coffee right out of the pot, plus fifteen seconds in the microwave. She doesn't like grape jelly or chocolate, and the last time she visited us, when she asked for a washcloth and I gave her one, she looked at it and said, "Don't you have a thinner one?"

Who in the world has a preference when it comes to the thickness of a washcloth?

My mother likes things a certain way, which makes her gratitude, simplicity, and appreciation all the more amazing.

When there is snow predicted in her area, I always call and ask if she has enough food—I know the answer already, but I still like hearing her say it.

"Oh, I have plenty," she says.

And she does. We all do.

In a world where we have a thousand TV channels and there is nothing on, when we look at a full refrigerator and say there's nothing to eat, when we walk through a house with games and books and sporting equipment and paper and pens and say there's nothing to do, we need to think like Velma thinks.

We need to see all the plenty.

Conclusion:

The Duck Book

For a while—not so much anymore—I used to receive "writer" presents as gifts. You know, weird stuff for Christmas and birthdays that writers are supposed to like. Over the years I was given many fancy pens, calendars of famous writers' desks, leather portfolios. I once received an engraved pewter pen holder with my monogram next to a quote about writing from Aristophanes—no, I didn't know who Aristophanes was; I had to look him up. But the pen holder still sits on my desk twenty years later.

But there was one Christmas—this was back when the kids were little—that I was given this thick, hardcover grammar reference book from my mother-in-law. Now, I can't tell you the title of this book, or even what its purpose was, but I clearly remember the white cover with the title above a single picture of a skinny yellow duck.

As soon as the wrapping paper was off this book, my son Alex, who was about five at the time, claimed it as his own. Alex carried the book around with him and referred to it when needed. In fact, if you asked him what he wanted for lunch, he would flip open the book and point to a page.

"According to this duck book," he'd say, "I want macaroni and cheese."

If you told Alex it was time for bed, he would show you a different page. "According to this duck book, I'm not tired."

And if you asked Alex who spilled the entire box of cereal on the floor and then tried to hide it behind the kitchen door, he would flip open the book and show you a different page. "According to this duck book," he'd say, "Nick did it."

In life, we have many duck books. We have friends. We have experiences. We have those who came before us, and we have ourselves. We have all the answers we ever need, provided we have the courage to ask the right questions.

According to our own duck book, we are good enough and clever enough and smart enough. We can take care of those we care about and we can accept care from those who care about us. We can live a life that we can be proud of and that can make others proud of us.

We can build something.

We can fix something.

And we can become something.

About the Author

Everett De Morier became a professional writer in 1994, when he sold a copy of his son's ultrasound picture along with an article entitled "My Wife Is Having the Reincarnation of Elvis" to *The Weekly World News*. For this, he received fifty dollars and a Bat Boy T-shirt.

De Morier has appeared on CNN, Fox News Network, NPR, and ABC, as well as in *The New York Times* and *The London Times*. He is the author of *Crib Notes for the First Year of Marriage: A Survival Guide for Newlyweds* and *Crib Notes for the First Year of Fatherhood: A Survival Guide for New Fathers*, both from Fairview Press.

De Morier has written seven original theatrical scripts, all produced by Cornerstone Drama of Dover, Delaware. His first novel, *Thirty-Three Cecils*, won the top fiction prize at the 2015 London Book Festival, is required reading in a New York high school, and is being developed into a major motion picture by Hornpin Media and Sunset River Productions.

De Morier was the keynote speaker at the 2016 Writers and Readers Conference in Delaware, where he was given a special recognition by Dover Mayor Robin Christiansen for his artistic contributions to the city and citizens of Dover. De Morier was also asked to speak at the Dover Art League event in 2017, where he was given a public tribute by Governor Jack Markell.

Everett De Morier lives in Dover, Delaware, with his wife and two children.